Nicolas has taught in primary schools in the UK for the past 20 years. In addition to having a Bachelor of Education Honours degree, he has a MBA and the National Qualification for Headship. Nicolas has trained in martial arts for the past 28 years, applying his discipline in the art of the physical fight, to help people realise their inner determination to fight cancer.

Nicolas Goldmeier

FIGHTING SPIRIT

A FIGHTER'S MINDSET IN HIS BATTLE AGAINST CANCER

AUSTIN MACAULEY
PUBLISHERS LTD.

A CIP catalogue record for this title is available from the British Library.

ISBN 9781786126658 (Paperback)
ISBN 9781786126665 (Hardback)
ISBN 9781786126672 (E-Book)

www.austinmacauley.com

First Published (2016)
Austin Macauley Publishers Ltd.
25 Canada Square
Canary Wharf
London
E14 5LQ

Acknowledgments

I thank God first and foremost, for giving me the gift of life and the ability to help others. I would like to thank my dear friend and mentor Steven, without whom the very concept of the 'Fighting Spirit' I would never have known. Also, I could not have written this book without the amazing encouragement of my dear wife, who is the one who encouraged me to put pen to paper. I thank my beloved parents for all their support and particularly my mother, who read through each and every word of the manuscript before I submitted it to the publishers. To my children, I offer my thanks, for all the tips and ideas they readily supplied. I am also indebted to all the health personnel; the doctors, nurses, surgeons, the specialist dentist who made my prosthesis, technicians, dieticians and porters, whose care and professionalism is second to none. I will always be eternally grateful to them. A big thank you, must also go to another one of my friends and mentors, Gabriel, for pushing me in my training to my very limits, but always taking the greatest of care with my delicate face.

To all these people I say, 'Thank you', I could not have written this book without you.

Foreword

The diagnosis of cancer has become the most feared by people of today's generation. As other diseases have become more curable, cancer remains stigmatised as a terminal illness, despite the significant advances in its ability to be managed and treated. Nicky Goldmeier's life was dramatically altered 15 years ago when, at the age of 26 and with a young family, he was diagnosed with cancer of the nasal sinus and plunged into a world of invasive medical treatment and faced with his own mortality.

I have known Nicky from the very start of his journey, as part of the Maxillofacial team responsible for his treatment. My role has been to provide the various prosthetic devices and on-going dental support to replace the teeth and parts of his mouth that needed to be removed by the aggressive surgery.

Cancer of the mouth impacts on many important functions of daily life. The chemotherapy and radiotherapy cause intense soreness of the mouth and throat. This can then lead to the mouth becoming permanently dry and restriction in opening. The surgery causes cosmetic issues and speech is often affected. The medical team involved in the treatment do everything they can to cure the disease and minimise the side effects, but it is likely that most patients will be left with some long-term deficiencies. However, these are the medical aspects that deal with the practical aspects of the process. It overlooks the psychological aspects of the treatment that every patient will have to struggle with, as they move from the diagnosis, through the treatment and the long-term aftermath.

Nicky's book 'Fighting Spirit' is about one man's experience and his development of inner strength, to help him combat both the disease and the treatment. He uses the mental powers he first learnt in martial arts, before diagnosis. Then, during the most difficult times of his initial diagnosis, the hospitalisation, recovery and recurrence of the disease, he expresses the importance to him of the power of his faith, the use of meditation techniques and strong support from family and friends. He illustrates these with analogous incidents from the Bible and the boxing world. He provides a powerful message to all, that this most challenging of diseases can be overcome, with an unwavering determination not to be beaten by, in boxing terms, this most fearsome of opponents.

This inspirational book, should be read not only by those whose lives have been affected by cancer, but all those involved in the treatment and the extended families, so that the importance of the mental attitude and the support of everyone involved, can be fully appreciated.

Dr Mark Barrett

Surgical Prosthodontist

UCLII Head & Neck Department

As a young man in his mid-teens and a keen martial artist, Nicky exuded enthusiasm when training and was quick to learn and master techniques. Having first met Nicky when we both attended a Kung Fu class in Edgware, I noted that he was exceptionally well mannered and polite; this was a credit to his parents, for as we say in my family, 'what's in the bone, comes out in the meat'. I also observed that when sparring (controlled fighting) in the class Nicky used his light frame to his advantage, through speed of movement, precision when executing a fighting technique and was just so difficult to corner.

Following me standing in for the Senior instructor in his absence and running the Edgware class, I was able to appreciate Nicky's ability to listen and learn regarding martial arts techniques and particularly fighting skills, which was an area that I specialised in. Nicky encouraged me to run my own class, and with his contagiously persistent enthusiasm, he introduced me to the Manager of a beautiful hall in Mill Hill. I walked along the centre of this hall, across newly varnished oak flooring and looking around me whilst inhaling the lovely smell of the treated wood, I thought, 'how could I turn this opportunity down'? I agreed to run a two-hour class every Monday evening from 7pm to 9pm, with my only stipulation being that all comers should be allowed to attend the class. This condition was immediately agreed to by the Manager of the hall.

With the help of Nicky, the class numbers quickly rose to over twenty with the youngest being 7years old whilst the eldest was 52. The two youngest members of my class were Nicky's youngest brother and his cousin, whom I affectionately nicknamed the two 'hit-men'. These two terrors forced me to quickly learn the technique of keeping my classes interesting and varied in order to maintain their focus.

During the years that I ran this class, I took great pleasure working with Nicky and developing his Kung Fu technique. He very quickly became not only a good friend, but also my right hand man in the class and would help the junior belts with their Kung Fu technique.

Whilst still a young man, Nicky was faced with some life changing challenges that many much more worldly people would struggle to cope with. I recall the day I received a telephone call from one of the students, informing me that Nicky (who was by then training to become a school teacher), had been the victim of a car accident, whilst on his way to undertake his first day of actual teaching experience. I felt my stomach tightening when I was then informed that he was in a coma. On my daily visits to see him in the hospital, I was encouraged (as others were) by his parents, to speak to him whilst he remained in a coma, in the hope that this might spark him back into consciousness. After a few days of nail-biting by his dear parents, we were all relieved when Nicky regained consciousness, although he initially was unable to speak or walk. I received a call from Nicky's parent who explained that he had written down, that he wanted to see me. I rushed over to the hospital to be greeted by the trademark Nicky smile – He was definitely back with us!

Within a few weeks of gaining consciousness, although unable to walk at that stage, Nicky was able to speak, and insisted on being a spectator during the running of his beloved Monday evening Kung Fu lesson.

Nicky was to recover from the car accident, go on to successfully achieve his black belt and eventually take over the running of the Mill Hill class.

A few years on, by which time Nicky was both a husband and a father, I received a message that he had been diagnosed with Cancer. I spoke to Nicky on the phone and he told me about the tumour in his face.

I recall shortly after this announcement, attending the wedding of a former student of my Mill Hill club. Nicky also attended this wedding, and it was clear that he was in severe discomfort following receiving what I believe was his first dose of chemotherapy and radiotherapy that same day.

I can say with confidence that Nicky is a modern day Gladiator, a fighting machine and a gentleman with deep beliefs and integrity. He has squared up to some major life challenges and has overcome them.

Nicky's account of his life's journey and his tenacity to overcome adversity, will not only hit you emotionally, but will inspire you.

Stephen (Friend and Martial Arts Instructor)

Prologue

The Force of the Fighting Spirit

I want to inspire you. I want to help guide you through circumstances that may seem impossible to overcome, but with a strong faith, coupled with an inner spirit of determination, you can overcome so much of what is put in your way. Do you want to know how? The 'Fighting Spirit'.

As I sheepishly entered the brightly lit hall, for what was to be my first taste of martial arts, I surveyed my surroundings. The décor on the walls and the ceiling. The shiny, smooth, but hard floor and of course the people who were all wearing martial arts suits, made up of coarse black trousers and white jacket-like tops, with an emblem in the corner next to the chest. Then there was the belt to top it all off; a range of colours, but most noticeably the black belts stood out, as I eyed these characters with a sense of caution and trepidation.

I made it through the first class, the second and the third and I began to feel less of a stigma attached to my clean white belt which hung around my waist. It was during the eighth or ninth martial arts class which I attended, that I had my first meeting with someone who would change my outlook on life, forever.

The class started as it always did, with a set of quick warm-up exercises, followed by stretching exercises that were always done with a partner. 'Nic, you pair up with him,' I heard my instructor say and as he pointed in someone's direction, I looked up and there in front of me was a tall, heavyweight figure of a man, with a large and muscular build and wearing a black belt. As he placed his leg on my shoulder, it felt like someone had put a sack of potatoes on to a rather flimsy shelf, hoping it would hold, but not honestly thinking it would. As I grimaced from the pressure the leg was putting on my shoulder, my partner introduced himself and I in turn told him my name, as I placed my comparatively matchstick leg on to his broad and muscular shoulder. 'Nice to meet you Steven.'

Steven is the kind of person who people warm to immediately and I was no exception, as we became life-long friends. Steven has a towering, gentle-giant-like stature, along with a face which exudes kindness and he has exceptionally good manners.

This makes Steven somewhat of an enigma when having to face him during a sparring session. One would not equate this gentle, kind, caring and polite human being, as one who was a heavyweight martial arts fighter, par excellence. I remember watching a video of him fighting two people at once and the way in which he had 'dealt' with the first person within the first ten seconds of the fight. I also recall a particularly enjoyable part of our training together, when we would stand facing each other, put our right shoulder leaning against the other's right shoulder and try to exert as much energy as possible, to push one another past a certain point, behind us on either side. I cannot recall anyone, ever pushing Steven backward, even one step. Although he certainly let us try!

Steven was a deadly fighter and could clearly distinguish between the art of fighting well and being caring and gentle when he didn't have a pair of boxing gloves on! He trained me as I went through all my 'belts' and achieved one colour after the next. I suppose the most daunting thing of all for me, was the actual fighting or free-sparing as we called it. At the end of each class, I would stand in front of my opponent, bow and then begin sparring, always with a sense of anxiety and nervousness.

The feeling of butterflies whirling around in my stomach, was a regular feature of free-sparing for me and try as I might, I simply couldn't get rid of this feeling, which was now becoming a feature of my preparation for battle! A regular feature, until one episode changed the way I sparred and in fact, the way I dealt with so many other things in my life. As I lined up to face, none other than, Steven himself, this tall, huge, muscular and in-shape figure of a man was looking down at me. The instructor gave the order to bow and then spar and as he did so, Steven said to me, 'Fighting spirit, Nicky...fighting spirit.' Those two words gave me the same strength, as would a gladiator being told that his opponent doesn't have a weapon. It was a message to me to keep going, keep pressing, keep moving and keep fighting, even when all odds are against you.

Those words meant so much to me at that moment and they have continued to help me carve my path through life's hurdles. I am a guy with a strong faith and I believe that there is someone watching over us, at all times. For reasons unbeknown to me, here was a friend, a mentor, who, unbeknown to him, was to be a guiding light and a source of inspiration through troubled times. Yes, Steven was often by my side through the hard times, but it was those words he uttered that evening as we trained and the same words which I would be told countless more times, which I was to take with me on my various journeys through the next 25 years. I regularly reminded myself, whatever comes my way, always remember the 'Fighting Spirit'.

The Tension Builds

Every time I had a shower I felt it. As I pressed my hand against my face I felt it. When I went to sleep at night I felt it and when I trained I felt it. 'It', was a small lump next to my nose and having that feeling of immortality that comes with being 26-years of age, I thought nothing of it. I had a wife and two young boys, aged two and four and they were, of course, the light of my life. I had also just completed two years of teaching and was moving on to a new job, which was effectively a promotion for me. Everything appeared great.

Until one day, that very small lump beside my nose became a very large, painful mass and I was desperate for help, for answers as to what this absurd swelling was. The right side of my face looked like it had been pounded again and again, leaving a huge swelling, redness and soreness. As I peered in the mirror, it looked like a couple of ping-pong balls had been stuffed into the right-hand side of my mouth. It must have looked very strange, to say the least and this extraordinary bulge caused me and my immediate family, extreme concern. Despite the anxiety felt by my wife, parents, brothers and sisters, none of us had 'cancer' high up on our list of potential ailments and that included my father; an experienced consultant doctor at a large London teaching hospital (although not in the field of oncology or Maxillofacial medicine).

Having gone to my dentist, then to the 'out-of-hours' GP, after which I went to Accident and Emergency at my local hospital, I was still none the wiser as to what this obscure and painful mass was on my face. The sensation I felt was one of a dull, but constant pain on the right side of my face, coupled with a numbness, which was to later set alarm bells ringing in the minds of the surgeons! Then some redemption, some relief from the absurd unknown, when my father managed to arrange an appointment with his consultant colleague and friend in Accident and Emergency.

I set off early in the morning and caught the Tube in to Central London and as I sat there, many negative thoughts began to race through my head, despite me trying to stay positive. I arrived at the hospital and introduced myself, following which I was pushed ahead of the queue (which I was relieved about, as it didn't give me any more 'free time' to ponder and mull over my adverse situation) and taken to have an X-ray. I may be wrong, but what I recall of that X-ray machine was that I had to sit ever so still, in front of a small screen for about 25 minutes. After the X-ray had ended, I turned to my father's colleague and asked him what he could see, to which his response was one of caution and careful consideration, although he looked concerned. To see a medical professional of such stature (he was a hugely experienced consultant) being concerned, filled me with an inner panic and dread which I bravely masked as he promptly referred me to the Maxillofacial Unit at another hospital nearby, to which I duly walked and sat waiting for my consultation. I was eventually summoned and I fearfully walked into the consultation room.

As a 26-year-old, who had never smoked or drank alcohol and had led a pretty healthy life (never been overweight and exercising regularly), I found myself in the hands of a couple of junior doctors, who curiously examined me and proceeded to tell me a whole list of possible diagnoses, which this swollen mass may be presenting. Being told this, just sent my mind in to a frenzy of 'what ifs...' and 'it could be...' but still nothing concrete. At last a consultant came into the room and greeted me and he must have seen the look of worry and despair on my face, which if faces could talk (without a mouth opening of course) would have said 'please, please, please, give me a definitive answer! Someone must know!'

In hindsight, I suppose they were being cautious, not wanting to rush to a conclusion or a possible diagnosis. They wanted to be sure as to what it was, without causing undue stress and concern. So, more anxiety and worry, the likes of which I have never experienced before and have never experienced since. It wasn't a question of 'Did I get the job?' or

'Did I get the required grades?' This was a case of 'Will I live…?' and 'What sort of life will I lead…? How will my life be changed…?' and 'How will it change the lives of those who love and care for me?' I left the hospital and headed home, with all these questions and more, weighing down on me, like a very dark cloud of pessimism hovering above.

'Thanks ever so much for seeing my son…' read the letter my father had just sent to the Maxillofacial Consultant. Of course the Consultant himself hadn't examined me and why should he have seen me? Twenty-six-years-old, non-smoker, good weight, exercises regularly, etc. etc. etc. But my parents were now worrying and rightly so.

I certainly don't blame the Consultant Surgeon for not taking a greater interest in my case. After all, he must have had hundreds of patients and due to my age and fitness levels, he was (in retrospect) quite right in delegating me and my 'lump' to a more junior doctor/surgeon. Nevertheless, he very kindly responded to my father's letter and subsequently looked at the X-rays, which had been sent from the first hospital and he duly phoned me.

I'll never forget that phone call, because I was in the middle of teaching a Year 3 class (aged seven-eight years), when a colleague walked in to my classroom. She appropriately informed me of a phone call, the nature of which was seemingly urgent and she took over from me in the classroom. Uneasily placing the phone receiver next to my ear, the Consultant told me that he would like to see me the following day, first thing in the morning. I stood silent for what seemed like an eternity, but can't have been more than 20 seconds and then thanked the surgeon and assured him that I would certainly be there first thing in the morning.

I travelled to the hospital by Tube, with my mother accompanying me. Each and every minute of that journey (and other similar journeys for the next couple of weeks) was torturous, as an anxiety built up inside me, about what my future would bring.

I arrived at the hospital and reported to the Maxillofacial reception desk, from where I was directed upstairs. The Registrar Surgeon came out to meet me and explained that we were waiting for a 'theatre slot' (obviously referring to the operating theatre), so that he could undertake the biopsy, removing a small amount of tissue from the right upper-side of my gum, just above the teeth. I waited and waited…and waited some more and still no sign of a vacant operating theatre. The wait only added to my levels of anxiety and tension, which would, unbeknown to me, only get worse.

Late into the afternoon, the surgeon informed me that there were still no free slots in the operating theatres and that he would have to perform the biopsy under local anaesthetic (LA). Initially, I was pleased that I didn't have to undergo a general anaesthetic for the first time in my life (again, ignorant of the fact that I would have quite a number of GAs in the coming months and years), but what I was about to experience, would have made me change my mind a thousand-fold.

The surgeon injected the LA in to my right upper gum, as would a dentist, about to perform a simple filling. He repeated this and then waited for the numbness to set in. He then began cutting, prodding and poking and I began to feel quite uncomfortable, but he removed the correct amount of tissue in a short time and closed up the cut with a couple of stitches. It was only after the procedure, that the pain in my mouth became excruciating, resulting in my overnight stay in hospital and being given a strong dose of pain killers to dull the pain. I barely managed to sleep through the night, with all kinds of thoughts racing around my mind, as well as the physical pain in my face and I was grateful to jump into a taxi the next morning and return home to those dearest to me. Once again, little did I know, that the road ahead was going to be a long and hard one.

The Fight Begins

I went back to the hospital a few days later to hear the conclusive results, only to be told that the results of the biopsy were unclear, although the doctors and surgeons thought that it was most likely to be something quite treatable. However, this initial optimism was short-lived, as a further histology test showed that the prognosis wasn't actually as positive as originally thought. The results of this new histology test were made known to the doctors and surgeons whilst I was on the train back home and only after I had stepped in to my house, was the news broken to me by my hysterical wife, as my two young boys were clutching at her ankles, unable to process the enormity of the moment.

I phoned the Consultant and he told me I had cancer in my sinus and nose and I was distraught, as well as being totally overwhelmed by my wife's reaction. The surgeons and doctors rallied together and with the help of a top ear, nose and throat surgeon at another London hospital, a treatment plan was devised. My cocooned world of 'living forever' had just been given an almighty blow, from which my naïve sense of immortality would (and rightly so) never recover. I was mortal and I had to muster all my fighting spirit to get through whatever the future would throw at me.

I knew nothing about cancer, because I was meant to be immortal. Cancer was for the elderly, for those who had already lived fulfilling lives. 'Why me?' I asked. But it's amazing how quickly you pull yourself together with, of course, faith and the support of friends and family. They came round to the house and they phoned me, offering words of support. Some didn't quite know what to say, but then that's quite normal. Until that point, I probably wouldn't have known what to say either. Then the phone rang and my mother picked up the receiver; 'It's Steven on the phone for you'. Steven had heard from other mutual friends, about my sorry state of affairs and rang me as a concerned friend would. However, Steven didn't sound concerned and as I placed the telephone against my ear, his ever so reassuringly deep and mellow voice simply said, 'Fighting spirit, Nicky, use the fighting spirit'.

At first, the doctors and surgeons were worried about the prognosis. They were concerned that the cancer had spread to the base of my brain, although my parents (and I now thank them for this), made a point of not telling me, because following further tests, the prognosis was, thank God, better and the oncologists and surgeons set about putting a treatment plan in place. I remember that the biggest dilemma was whether the cancer should first be removed, followed by chemo and radiotherapies or the other way around. They subsequently all agreed that they would blast the tumour and shrink it in size, resulting in an easier, less obtrusive operation to remove it.

So the day came, when I was admitted to hospital as an inpatient, to undergo the first round of medicinal concoctions. I was put on a drip, containing a concoction of chemotherapy drugs for a week and underwent daily radiotherapy, simultaneously. This all started on the Monday morning and by the Friday my mouth felt like it had been set on fire, over and over again. A bit like sunburn, but inside the mouth and it was from this moment on, that I well and truly attached myself to the belief that I would never give up. I had the 'fighting spirit' and whilst those around me were very supportive and my faith was now stronger than ever, I had to show grit and determination and a positive sense of stubbornness, to keep fighting. To stand in front of this cancer and fight with confidence that, please God, all would be well. Fighting spirit…fighting spirit.

As well as the chemotherapy drugs, administered over the course of a week's stay in hospital, I was also given a different chemo drug as a day patient. This, in itself, came with its own potential complications, as the particular drug given to stop my arch enemy, also had the potential to affect my kidneys. So, a bag of saline was first flushed through my system and only once I had been to the toilet to pass water a few times, did the nurses put the bag of drugs on to the drip stand.

The few days in hospital became increasingly difficult, as it was terribly lonely and I wasn't able to eat much as the medication burnt my mouth and throat. Good friends and family would bring me food that was easier for me to eat and was either soothing on my mouth or certainly didn't hurt as much as most of the other foods I had tried and which was on offer in the hospital. My older brother used to visit me very late at night and I would fight my tiredness to stay up to see him, both for the company and the soup he would bring with him from one of my favourite restaurants.

The fight with this dreaded disease was not just with the medication and longing, urging, wishing for the big C to be gone, but also being in this large hospital, on a ward where, although they made me feel welcome and gave the best care possible, I felt isolated and away from the community and people to whom I was closest.

Every evening, at about 10pm, when my family (not my older brother, as he paid me a welcomed visit much later on in the evening, at about midnight!) got up to leave, I would accompany them downstairs with my drip (containing the ever so important chemotherapy drug) to the front doors of the hospital. I kissed them and bade them farewell and as they walked out of sight, my heart would always sink, as my loneliness allowed my mind to conjure up a plethora of possibilities of what the future might bring for me.

This solitude requires an enormous amount of fighting spirit, a way of attaching oneself to something spiritual, to a superpower I call God and which others might refer to as an ultimate power. For me, there was no hesitation, as I quickly learnt to adjust from the human company I experienced through most of each day, to the otherworldly and Divine company, which my faith had ensured was built-in to my psyche. So, the 'fighting spirit' was probably quite an apt name for my on-going battle with this treacherous disease, as this fight was not only physical, but had a large proportion of spirituality attached to it.

The highlight of my mornings, during my stays in hospital, was a regular visit from the 'fighting spirit' man himself, Steven. On his way to work, Steven would come up to the ward and help me eat breakfast. After a lonely night, where continuous sleep was rarely a possibility, my good friend Steven would chat to me, help me eat my breakfast and continuously remind me of the need to keep focused on the 'fighting spirit', the battle I was in the midst of, to evict this unwanted tenant from my face. Having spent a week in hospital having chemo and radiotherapy, the battle was well and truly on.

The 'Spirit' of the Fight

Until this day (some 15 years later) I am not entirely sure whether or not those around me were truly able to understand the 'fighting spirit' I was focused on. They were always there for me and cared for me like never before. I felt a strange sense of security, with the knowledge that all around me cared for me so much. But the fight was ultimately my own and when I ventured into some ever so supportive sessions of meditation, the front line of battle had just moved a step closer in my fight to defeat this concealed enemy. I was encouraged to visualise the cancer as an enemy being attacked by all my healthy blood cells, which I pictured as laser blasters from *Star Wars*, each time weakening the enemy and slowly watching it wane and fade. This visualisation became such a crucial tool in my fight. The mind can do great things and I had been successfully taught by a meditation expert, how to visualise the fight against this dark enemy so much so, that the term 'fighting spirit' now took on a sort of concrete image, one that I would use in the coming months.

At the end of the first week in hospital, my drip was detached from me and I slowly walked down the stairs (I had to use the lift all week, because of the drip) with a couple of good friends who had come to take me home. As I sat in the front passenger seat of the car, I started worrying about the food I wasn't able to eat. It wasn't like I was some gigantic, obese person who had weight issues anyway and was conveniently losing a bit of weight in the process of trying to fight cancer. No, for me, a lightweight (soon to become a flyweight!), the prospect of losing weight made me all the more nervous. As we drove past shops, I asked my friends if I could buy some yoghurt to try out. They parked the car and ran into a shop to buy it. As I opened the carton, with baited breath at the prospect of trying some unfamiliar, as yet untried food, I hesitated and put the smallest amount of yoghurt into my mouth. The pain was so excruciating, it felt like someone had peeled my mouth with a potato peeler and rubbed salt in to the raw wounds.

Nevertheless, I kept the pain to myself until I stepped into my parents' home, where I was going to stay for the next few weeks.

It was only through trialling different foods and drinks, that I was able to determine that the menu I was going to have to endure over the coming weeks was water, watercress soup and soya yoghurts. Not much of a selection, but one which I became used to, as these foods (and water) didn't hurt my mouth and throat and gave me at least some kind of nutrition, along with the high energy drinks which also, miraculously, didn't cause me any discomfort.

As the days and weeks of radio and chemotherapy went on, my mouth and throat became increasingly sore and unbearable, to the extent that I was put on quite a high dose of oral Morphine. When fighting through something, whatever it is, you cannot simply ignore and disregard the seemingly supplementary tools at your disposal. When a fighter prepares themselves, they eat the appropriate foods, the protein and high energy culinary delights, which provide them with the stamina to keep fighting, to keep going past the threshold. This was what the morphine was to me; an extra tool by which I could face up to my opponent with a degree of solidity, whereby I could remain focused on the task in hand. It was almost like an officer regrouping his platoon at the end of a day and reminding them of the fight ahead. I guess it is difficult to do this when under a barrage of gun fire and heavy artillery. So I too, (with the aid of the morphine) was given a haven of respite that enabled me to prepare for the continued fight.

I started radio and chemotherapy at the end of July and by the end of October it was completed and it was at this point that I was reminded of the aim of the treatment I had just endured. One of the objectives was to shrink the cancer, so that the surgery would be made easier and less invasive. So during the months of August, September and most of October, I could really focus on the fight, as well as the 'spirit' part and I would summon my spiritual energies to reinforce the more conventional forms of battle.

Daily Radiotherapy

Most people associate masks with clowns, the stage or a disguise of some sort. As I was prepared for radiotherapy, the radiographers had to make me a mask, so that clear and accurate markings could be drawn on to it and therefore, guide the treatment to precisely where the disease was located. The mask was made of transparent plastic and fitted my face with precision. This accuracy was achieved by using layer upon layer of plaster of Paris and then moulding it in to a mask.

Every time I had radiotherapy, I would go down to the hospital's basement (where the radiotherapy treatments were all carried out) and wait my turn. I never had to wait very long at all and I would be escorted down a slope to the treatment room. I would climb on to a table and lie down, facing upwards. Then the mask would be put on to my face and secured to the table so as not to allow a single movement, lest the radiation not hit the points with accuracy.

In addition to this, I was told that the radiation could potentially, seriously damage my eyes. So as to protect my eyes, a thin piece of lead metal, which looked much like a pencil one would use for writing, was placed on a flat screen of clear plastic, about a metre and a half away from my face and directly above it. 'You must look straight at the pencil, all the time,' is what I was told in a very clear voice by one of the radiographers. At first, this sounded easy and such a simple task to deter any hazards to my eyesight. But as I stared at the 'lead pencil', balancing above my head, it disappeared! I realise, of course, that it hadn't really disappeared, but as I kept watch of this piece of metal, the illusion of it vanishing, took place each and every time I had radiotherapy. It wouldn't have usually caused me any concern, but I was relying on actually looking at this 'lead pencil', as a sure way of protecting my vision. This experience wasn't of course painful, it was just annoying and very uncomfortable (and in retrospect, quite amusing!).

Yet another fight had started to unravel and I was determined to stay on top of it again. It was a few minutes into the treatment, when I smelt a nauseous, overpowering smell. The best way to describe this smell is, if you are out walking along a very busy street in London, on a very hot summer's day and you pass a bus. The fumes from that bus would overpower you and you would automatically raise your hand to your mouth, to cover it. Well, it was a smell very similar to that, but this time I was simply unable to cover my mouth, or nose for that matter. I started to feel sick. What if I was sick, laying pinned down, unable to even move my head to the side, just in case? I could quite easily have given up at this point, but I was now so entrenched in my battles, which I was now fighting on a number of different fronts, I was determined. I left the hospital with my friend, who had so kindly driven me on a daily basis and walked into a chemist. 'Do you have any oil of cloves?' I asked. 'Sure,' came the reply and the pharmacist duly bagged and gave me the oil.

The following day, before going down to the basement for radiotherapy, I poured the oil on to a tissue and on to my sleeve and as I climbed on to the radiotherapy treatment table, I felt more at ease with my newly found and prepared ammunition. It's amazing how many millions of pounds and dollars countries spend on developing new weapons and yet the new addition to my arsenal cost me only a couple of pounds. I know it is very different, but this was my big battle and I would use any weapon available!

The Mysterious Healer – Using the Inspiration of Visualisation

My two boys, now both young men, have always had a passion for films and can pick up lines said by characters, in very quick time. At one stage, they would watch martial arts films over and over again and not only did they practise the moves they saw, they would say the key lines (quite understandably, having watched the film so many times), with a similar intonation to the way they had actually been said by the actors. They once picked up a couple of lines from a martial arts film and although I simply cannot remember which film, or even the context of the dialogue, the dialogue began with the words, 'Be calm, at peace with yourself...' This statement is a typical axiom said by many martial artists from the countries who follow the martial arts, as a guide to life itself and as violent as these arts may seem, anyone with a little knowledge of these, will tell you how huge is the discipline and control needed to remain focused and execute the carefully mastered moves.

As soon as I had been diagnosed with cancer, my father contacted a gentleman who ran 'visualisation' sessions for all kinds of people, including those who were unwell.

The day after speaking to John on the phone, I had my first taste of 'visualisation'. (As I mentioned in a previous chapter, I was taught how to visualise the cancer by meditating on it.) John was a kind and friendly character who had travelled to distant lands to learn the art of meditation and visualisation and had deployed all he had learnt on the very grateful clients with whom he had spent quality time. The doorbell at my parents' home rang and I accompanied John into the living room and we both sat down opposite each other. He spoke in a calm and serene voice, taking time to explain his methodology and commenting from time to time, on the vast display of books that sat on the shelves from ceiling to floor in my parents' living room.

We chatted for a while, about the experiences I had endured thus far and then he closed his eyes with me and took me through a series of visualisation exercises. I imagined the cancer as a dark, unwanted enemy, which had trespassed into parts of my body and needed to be removed. I pictured all my healthy blood cells forming a huge army, using all their weaponry and physical might against this uninvited and malignant army of cells and driving them further and further backwards into oblivion. In later years, the words '…be calm, at peace with yourself…' come to mind when I think about the sessions I had with John and there were only two activities in which I would genuinely feel calm and at peace. One was when I said a prayer, to ask for a complete recovery from the cancer and the other was when I was with John, exploring places and visualising the utter defeat of the tumour, which would raise my feelings of optimism to the heights of a soaring eagle, gliding, floating on the wind.

As well as being another much needed companion during these days of helplessness and frustration, I believe that my sessions with John were not only helpful in relaxing and calming me, but that they actually had a positive role to play in physically destroying and evicting the cancerous cells from my body. I believe that the mind, the inner spirit, is very powerful and can be channelled to do great things, if focused and determined. After all, why would being 'calm and at peace' help someone who was going to fight a very physical battle, using punches, kicks, throws, chops, knees, etc.? Ask any boxer, any martial artist, any fighter who is disciplined and they will all tell you, that aggression must be controlled and that the mind, that inner spirit, can be very powerful when used appropriately and effectively.

Indeed, you could ask any meditation expert and they will vouch for the mysterious power of the mind. Although, perhaps the most mysterious thing of all was that, following my sessions with John, he was never heard from or seen again. My father and I tried in vain to search for him, to thank him for the amazing support and opportunity he had given me, but to no avail. John was one of my guardian angels and I will always be grateful to him.

The Obturator – A Prosthetic Mouth-Piece

A couple of months after the chemotherapy and radiotherapy had finished, I was back in hospital. I had always been told that these treatments would probably not completely remove the cancer; they would shrink it and therefore make it more easily operable. It was a Sunday evening and as I ate my supper, I realised that eating would never be the same again, following the next day's operation and it never has been!

The fight until now had been harsh, as any fight against a mysterious enemy would be, but now I was preparing for a more 'physical fight'.

The Consultant Surgeon had taken me through the steps of the surgical procedure and described, as best he could, what the resultant effects would be. I can assure you, that I couldn't really visualise quite what the surgeon was describing to me, but I was told that part of my hard palate would be removed, as well as all my upper teeth on the right side of my face. The sinus, together with the tumour, would be taken out, along with bones from inside my nose. I was to be left with a cavity from my mouth to my right eye. I heard what the surgeon was saying, but I simply couldn't get my head around it. How would I eat and drink and how would I speak? 'We'll make you a mouth-piece, which will enable you to eat, drink and speak,' said the ever so kind surgeon, as if he could read my mind.

I remember so clearly, how I held my wife's hand tight, as the kindly porter wheeled me, as I lay on my bed, down to the operating theatres. I vividly recall the feelings of despair I felt when we had reached a certain point, as my wife was told that she could come no further. I felt a sense of nervousness as she disappeared out of sight.

After eight hours in the operating theatre, with my mother and wife waiting for me by my hospital bed, praying, along with hundreds, if not thousands, of well-wishers from around the globe, for a positive outcome, I was taken to the intensive care unit (ICU) and remained there overnight, to be monitored. All I can remember of that experience in intensive care, was one of the nurses telling me that she needed to remove my catheter, which was helping me to urinate unaided. I would usually have been terribly embarrassed, but I was so oblivious to my surroundings, that I remember feeling only the pain as it was removed, but no feelings of awkwardness or shame.

The next morning I was taken to the Maxillofacial ward and until then, I had been kept heavily sedated. Now that I was back on a regular ward, I slowly came around and as I did so, I could feel the huge amount of bruising all over my face. It felt puffed up and I delicately prodded my cheeks, mouth and nose, as I slowly made my way to the bathroom to look in the mirror. As I looked back at myself, I looked a sorry sight, as my nose (usually quite thin) was huge. There were big bruises under my eyes and my cheeks were enlarged to about three times their normal size.

I looked like I had been in the ring with a heavyweight boxer for ten rounds and in fact, when a friend came to the hospital the day after the operation, he walked up to me, asked me how I was and then promptly left. I recall so vividly, that at that very moment, I was feeling terribly sick and nauseous and I remember being so thankful that this friend hadn't stayed, as I didn't know him that well and I would have felt uncomfortable. Years later, he explained to me that he left so abruptly because he was completely taken aback by the sight with which he was met. He simply couldn't cope with seeing me in that state, hence he expressed his good wishes and quickly left the hospital.

Once I was fully awake and aware of my surroundings and what I had endured (when I was first taken back to the ward), I felt with my tongue, the piece of metal which now acted as my hard palate and right-hand side teeth. The surgeons soon spoke to me on their round of the ward and explained what they had done and I thanked God and them, of course.

The surgeons clearly explained that the operation was a success and they had removed all the cancer, although they had only taken one millimetre of clear tissue around the tumour, whereas usually they like to take three. However, (as they continued) they would have needed to remove my right eye permanently, in order to take the normal three millimetres of clear tissue. In the words of those medical professionals, 'We decided to take the gamble...'

Now came the massive hurdle of eating, drinking and speaking. I found eating and drinking a real challenge; I felt so depressed that I could no longer eat as before, I could no longer drink as before and the foreign body in my mouth would really take some getting used to. Of course I knew that this was a small price to pay for the removal of the cancer, but I felt anxious and vulnerable; a sense of not being in control anymore. The mouth-piece was obviously very real, tangible; a solid piece of metal with teeth on, inside my mouth and only strong determination and will-power would help me overcome my newly constructed mouth.

Getting used to speaking with the obturator in my mouth, was the easiest part of the three (eating, drinking and speaking), although there were also obstacles to overcome with this element as well. Take, for example, trying to pronounce a letter 'P' and a letter 'B', without the use of a fully functioning hard palate. If the mouth-piece wasn't fully functioning, air would come through my nose and mouth and create a muffled sounding 'B' or 'P' and this was extremely frustrating. I envisioned speaking to people who didn't know that I was wearing a mouth prosthesis and pictured the expression on their faces when they couldn't understand what I was saying.

To be perfectly honest, whilst I have become so accustomed to eating, speaking and drinking with my obturator in my mouth, doing these three things will always cause me concern. But, when all is said and done, it's a small price to pay. Although I may well have to toil with my mouth-piece, I would much rather live with the knowledge, that the faculties which are so essential to my mouth, are being continuously aided rather than the death sentence which cancer so often brings.

Jacob's Fight with an Angel

The famous biblical episode of Jacob's struggle with the guardian angel of his brother Esau, describes how Jacob was permanently scarred in his dispute with his brother, yet arch-enemy, who relentlessly pursued him, angered by the deal he had made to exchange his birthright for a pot of lentil soup.

Having just left the company of his brother Esau, Jacob, together with his entire family, continued on their travels, allowing Esau to make his own way with his family, to a completely different location. A little while after setting out on their journey, Jacob realised that he had forgotten to bring some of the utensils used to make food for the family.

He therefore returned to collect the articles he had left behind and as he was in the process of gathering his belongings, he was confronted by the guardian angel of Esau, who (judging by Esau's ruthless attitude towards his brother) clearly wanted to destroy Jacob and his family. After a long night of wrestling and Jacob receiving a blow to his thigh, which would leave him with a permanent injury and a limp, Jacob grabbed hold of the angel who pleaded with Jacob to let him go. In desperation, the angel told Jacob that it was his turn to praise God up in the heavenly spheres and he implored with Jacob to let him go, so he could perform his service of praise. But Jacob was unmoving in his refusal to let the angel go. He was only willing to release this menace, this perilous individual, if he was to bless him. So desperate was the angel to get back for his 'heavenly slot', that he did bless him, by changing Jacob's name to Israel.

So the angel leaves Jacob with a legacy, a new name by which an entire nation will be called. 'The Children of Israel'. Henceforth, the Jewish people are not (in the majority of cases) referred to as 'The Children of Abraham' or indeed 'The Children of Isaac', but as 'The Children of Israel'.

The battles I have fought with this oncogenic enemy have indeed left me scarred, both physically and emotionally. To deny that I had come out the other end completely unscarred would be a blatant lie and I do not believe anyone who goes through an experience such as having cancer, is ever truly free of the physical and emotional wounds it leaves behind. But just as Jacob would never fully recover from the blow to his thigh, which left him with a permanent limp, he made sure (before releasing his foe) to gain something from his traumatic experience. So too, was I determined to gain from my epic battle.

What was my blessing? I assure you that it was not a change of name and I am definitely not a leader of a nation. My blessing was threefold. Before the radiotherapy and chemotherapy treatments started, the doctors told me that I was in danger of not being able to father any more children, as there was a possibility that the radiation and the potent chemotherapy drugs could affect my fertility. Yet I had two more beautiful children and in addition, I consider it a blessing that I am able to give hope to others, who are going through a similar experience. Most importantly, I view it as a further benediction that the experiences of cancer have taught me to appreciate life, like never before.

My struggle with cancer has left me scarred (physically and emotionally), but like the biblical character Jacob, I also gained so much from the fight. I did not let the cancer get away with it so easily, to simply leave me with my own personal 'limp'. I had fought too hard to do that and I wanted something in return. The inner 'fighting spirit' which had kept me going during my struggle, would turn to the enemy and insist on it leaving me, but not without paying the price of giving me a positive legacy, by which I could continue living a continuously fulfilling life.

Neck Dissection

Following the weeks of radio and chemotherapy and the further weeks it took to slowly wean myself off the high doses of morphine I was given to dampen the pain, I had regular scans and check-ups from both the oncologists and Maxillofacial surgeons. On one of my visits to one of these truly praiseworthy professionals, the surgeon felt my neck, as is common practise following a diagnosis of head and neck cancers. As he ran his fingers across my neck, pushing gently to feel for any rogue glands, he stopped. He felt again and again. My heart started to beat faster at the very real, but truly unthinkable, prospect of what he may be about to tell me and tell me he did! 'I can feel a gland that is not right and I'd like to send you for a cytology test.' I didn't really need to ask him what this was, because of the care they always took to explain things as clearly as they could.

There were always those pleasurable occasions after a gruelling three hour martial arts training session, when I would step in to a steaming shower, bathe and nurse my aches and pains, get in to my pyjamas and then sit down in front of the television with a bowl of warm soup and just relax. I had given my all, trained hard, focused and I felt a sense of achievement.

This is what I felt following the rigour of the radiotherapy and the pain of the chemotherapy. Now suddenly, in my comparative state of relaxation, I was being told 'You may have to get up and fight again.'

I went to have the cytology test and lay down on the bed, following which the doctor carefully placed a needle, attached to a syringe, into my neck and very carefully and precisely, withdrew some of the fluid which was to be sent to the pathologists for testing. Once again, the agony and despair I experienced whilst waiting for the cytology results was almost palpable, with a sense of awareness of what the outcome would be. But I always had my faith and of course the 'fighting spirit', both of which would see me through these unsympathetic days of waiting. A couple of days later I went back to the hospital for the results. The surgeon called me in to his room and gently and kindly broke the wretched news to me, for the second time in my life. Indeed, I did have cancer on the right-hand side of my neck. But once a fighter has experienced a blow, a punch or a kick, they are always prepared and organise themselves accordingly. So I prepared myself once more, for what I had hoped I would never have to prepare for again.

I remember training in martial arts on consecutive nights of the week and the feeling of stiffness and fatigue from one hard training session to the next, but at least I had the twenty-four-hour gap, in which to recover slightly. However, this unexpected and rather sudden revelation that I now had cancer in my neck, did not give me the 'twenty-four-hour reprieve' which I had enjoyed when training. I felt like I had been given no time at all, to prepare for the next onslaught. But once again, God helps those who help themselves and I mustered the 'fighting spirit' which I now identified with, as a natural ally and I prepared for battle.

Like the battles before, this was a very physical battle, with pain and discomfort, the likes of which I had never experienced before. The severe pain was made very real, when one evening, a nurse came to change one of the drains which I had in my neck, helping to drain any unwanted fluid from the site of the surgical procedure. As she carefully pulled the plastic tube from my wound, a technique she must have done countless times, it honestly felt like someone had their hands wrapped tightly around my neck and was viciously squeezing my trachea. I felt like I was being strangled! Until this day, I still cannot find words to describe with accuracy, the immense agony and pain I felt at that moment.

In total, forty four glands on the right-hand side of my neck had been completely removed. The surgeons had made a vertical incision down the right-hand side of my neck and then horizontally across my neck, to enable them to reveal all the glands and take out what they felt was necessary. I even had battle scars to show what I had been through, as I had staples going down and then across my neck. When a fighter has battle scars, be it a black eye or other bruising to various parts of their combat-ridden body, I'm guessing that they feel the same way I did, very proud (especially if they have won the fight; but even if they haven't). Here I was, having been through an operation to, once again, remove a foreign and unwanted mass from my body and I had these 'staples' to prove it. I guess some people would shy away from showing these somewhat obscure post-operative 'things' to the outside world, but not me. I had fought a tough battle to get this far and I was going to (literally) hold my head up high.

Of course people looked, some even stared at me (it was quite a shocking sight to behold), but all I wanted to do was to sit people down and tell them my story thus far. Of course I didn't, but it was the feeling of wanting to, which made me feel a bit like a hero. A Mohammed Ali, Lennox Lewis, Mike Tyson, Evander Holyfield figure, who had just been presented with the world title crown, after a gruelling fight.

During my week in hospital, recovering from the 'neck dissection', the surgeons told me that they had removed all the potentially affected glands. I went back to the hospital a few days later and the consultant looked surprised and took several minutes, before he told me the news that they had found cancer in the centre of only one gland. I looked heavenward, towards my ultimate 'corner-man' and thanked the one who had and still does, give me the ability to fight.

Once You Have Heard it, Nothing will Faze You

It was three months after the cancer had been removed from the right side of my neck (44 nodes in total), followed by radiotherapy to mop up any microscopic bits, that I had an MRI and CT scan. I had been told that I was to have these scans every three months for the first couple of years following my diagnosis.

Even as early on as June 2000, I had learnt to always take a friend or family member with me, to consultations at which I was to be given scan results. What I was subsequently told, nothing could prepare me for. It's strange, because of all I had been through up until then, I would have expected to react differently, but I didn't. The Specialist Registrar sat me down with my sister sitting beside me. 'I'm sorry Nicky, it looks like the cancer has returned.' I don't know why, but it was almost unbelievable. Perhaps, once one has endured what I had faced over the past year, one somewhat believes it cannot happen again in such close proximity to the last time. But here I was, being told that the disease I had fought to be rid of, had returned.

I looked at my sister and she looked at me, both of us dumbstruck. My wife was pregnant with the child we had been blessed with and were told might be difficult to conceive (due to all the treatment I had endured) and now I was being told that this dark enemy had returned. 'We did tell you Nicky, that if we didn't remove your eye, we were taking a gamble; I'm afraid it hasn't paid off...' Hardly reassuring. These words caused my heart to race and left me feeling slightly bewildered, as if in another time and place; almost surreal.

As I arrived home, I was determined to do all I could to fight this nemesis, if that was what the biopsy proved it to be and I was almost sure it was. But somewhere in the back of my mind, I was praying, hoping, pleading that it wasn't the return of my adversary. But once again, this was not a physical fight of any shape or form, but a fight whose ammunition is hope and prayer and a strong desire that the results of the forthcoming biopsy would be only good.

As had now occurred so often, I was driven to the hospital and went straight upstairs to the Maxillofacial ward. I was shown to my bed and slowly perused the other patients in the ward, as I also familiarised myself with the staff I had come to know over the past few months. I settled in, as best anyone can settle in to a hospital ward and I sat melancholy at the end of my bed, thinking and trying to rationalise this latest episode in my life. My rationalising turned into more of a conversation with my Higher Power. After all I had gone through thus far, I was pleading, beseeching for a positive outcome to this latest chapter in the roller coaster of events of the last few months.

As I awoke early on the Monday morning and savoured those first ten waking seconds of serenity, I was greeted by a nurse and the surgeon who did all the relevant tests, before I was taken down to the operating theatre. As I was wheeled into the room in which they always seemed to administer the general anaesthetic, the anaesthetist recognised me and kindly said 'Nice to see you again' and placed a mask over my face. That is all I remember.

Back on the ward I quickly gathered my thoughts, after all, it had only been a short procedure and once again, I directed my attentions to the divine, otherworldly Higher Power of mine, for some sense of tranquillity and calmness. As the evening approached, I felt a sense of restlessness at being cooped up in a hospital ward and advanced towards one of the friendly surgeons who was doing that evening's ward round. I asked him if my father could come and pick me up; if it was alright for me to leave the hospital. He hesitated and asked me a question. 'If you can answer this question, you can definitely go home,' he said. 'Who is the President of Russia?' came the question and I answered (almost immediately), 'It's Putin.' He presently loaned me his mobile phone and told me to call my father to ask him to pick me up.

Having had the biopsy on the Monday, I went back to the hospital with my father, to hear the histology results from the consultant a few days later on the Friday. I waited in a rather busy and hectic outpatients waiting room and prayed, yearning for the results to be good and I would regularly speak to my Higher Power and yearn for those results to show nothing which would be troublesome. As if in a dream world at that moment, I heard the receptionist telling me to go for a short walk and return in about 30 minutes, when the outpatient department would be less busy.

So my father, being an academic and an avid reader, headed, with me, straight towards a well-known book store and we went inside. I wasn't really in the mood to read anything at that moment in time but, as well as my father, I browsed the book-laden shelves, in the hope of finding a source of motivation and encouragement. I picked up a book which I had spotted because of its significant title, presenting itself as a self-help book on the ups and downs of life and opened it randomly. The title jumped out of the page at me, 'How to Cope with Fear'. I read the chapter and digested as much as I could in the short time I had in the store, until my father signalled to me that it was time to leave and head back to the hospital.

As I walked back to the hospital, then sat waiting for the few minutes before seeing the consultant (the department had significantly emptied during the time my father and I had been in the book store), I thought about the short chapter on fear and the indelible impression it had left on my mind. It had given me a boost of extreme positivity, as we were called in to the surgeon. I held my breath and waited. There was a pause. The surgeon looked at a piece of paper, scanning its contents and then he told me. He told me that it was indeed, nothing; just a shadow on the scan's images. I was elated, jubilant, and euphoric. I can't quite describe the relief, but being a man of faith, I cast my eyes heavenward and said thank you in a whisper, which was said with so much passion and feeling, that it might well have been heard clearly across the world. So, every time I have a scan, I take nothing for granted. I am ready for the potential feelings of fear and dread of whatever I am told, but I have the strongest faith that it will be good. Why? It is because I am a fighter and fights do not always need to be physical. Perhaps the most difficult of all fights to win are those where your enemy remains elusive and hidden, but keeping this hidden foe away, will always be my fight. A fight I am prepared to live with, not die for.

Battling with Emotions - Am I Hurting Them?

I'll never forget the kindness of one of the nurses on the Maxillofacial ward during one of my stays in hospital (although every single one of them always displayed a huge amount of care and support). It was late at night and she had just finished her round of seeing to patients' needs and dimmed some of the lights, so that the patients could get some half-decent sleep (I could never sleep soundly in hospital and I guess I am not the only one!), when she stopped by my bedside.

I had just noticed one of the two photographs of my wife and two children which I had brought with me for my hospital stay and I was holding it in my hand. As I gazed at the photo, a plethora of emotions raced through my mind. I was about to fall into the dangerous mind tricks syndrome, when the mind often seizes the opportunity of the situation (the loneliness, the quiet, being in hospital and fearing for the future), when the nurse asked me if everything was OK, as I looked longingly at the photo of my wife and two young boys. I had brought the photo with me as a means of some emotional support, for my latest stay in hospital, but was reluctant to look at it too often, fearing that I would just break down with emotion. 'They're really lovely,' she said with a soft and compassionate tone and I was silent, thinking about how my illness had affected the people closest to me and the emotions they were going through.

I'm pretty sure that this kind-hearted nurse said nothing to me after that, but she just stayed with me for a few minutes, long enough to enable me to think about those in the photo and then she slowly walked away from my bed and attended to other patients' needs. But in that moment, that time of contemplation, my determination to be strong was reinforced. In a peculiar way, my strong emotions for those I loved so dearly were all part of the overall fight. To recover for them and to stay strong through everything for them, was a big part of the fight.

Everyone Needs an Adrian

So as to explain, as clearly as I can, how those near and dear to a person are so much a part of the fight, I am reminded of one of my favourite series of films: *Rocky*. These films are about a boxer who has a vision and a dream, that one day he will be the heavyweight champion of the world. Rocky sets out in life with very little, but finds himself a trainer and then meets a girl with whom he falls in love. Both his trainer, Mickey and his girlfriend (who he subsequently marries) stick by him, through his training regime (including moments of bad temper and frustration) and his competitive fights.

Certainly, in the first four films when we meet Adrian, Rocky Balboa's ever suffering, but exceptionally loyal wife, it becomes clear that the relationship between these two characters is one of love, devotion and loyalty. Adrian clearly doesn't like her husband being punched in the ring and would probably do whatever she could to stop Rocky being hurt so brutally for the sake of sport, but she knows that it is his passion and he has a dream to fulfil. We are continually reminded, throughout the films, of his deep passion for boxing and his quest to become heavyweight champion of the world and to keep that status for as long as he can.

As the seconds are counted down to the end of each of Rocky's bouts, the viewer senses that he is thinking about the one true love in his life and as the final bell is sounded, he calls out to his wife, with a heartfelt cry, 'Adrian! Adrian!' In a frantic voice, which is clearly being drowned out by all the commotion going on, in and around the ring, Rocky screams his wife's name and because of their connection and their dedication to each other, Adrian climbs into the ring, desperate to get to her husband. To hold him and reassure him, that through thick and thin, she will always be there. Despite Rocky's face having been battered and bruised, sometimes beyond recognition, she still shows her feelings of immense love and dedication to him.

We all need our own "Adrian", so that at the end of each fight, we can call out to them and they will always be there for us. In my case, I had many people who I thought of when coming round after a general anaesthetic, experiencing immense pain or when spending lonely nights on a hospital ward. Of course, there were individual people who were always first on my mind (my parents, brothers, sisters, children, wife and close friends) and who made the overall fight that bit easier. These people were my "Adrian".

Then there was Mickey, Rocky's loyal and unfaltering trainer, in whom he put his trust and looked up to as a role-model and mentor. In fact, when Mickey dies in the third film, having been ruthlessly pushed by Rocky's opponent, Rocky's display of mourning is so heartfelt and a sight usually only reserved for a close relative. My friend, Steven, is my mentor and my role-model and he is most certainly alive and well. His unwavering loyalty and commitment to keeping the 'fighting spirit' forever alive within me, even during my darkest times, will continuously be treasured.

The Relief After a Painful Stretch

All the martial arts classes I have ever attended have had a very clear structure to them, from the start to the finish, utilising every moment to the full. A certain amount of time is apportioned to warming up, a definite time schedule is given to perfecting the age-old moves of the specific art of fighting to ensure they are flowing, powerful and deliberate and then some time is allotted to free-sparring. One of the most important features of any martial arts training which involves kicks, are the stretching exercises which are usually done following the initial warm up. By stretching the body, particularly the legs, in as varied a way as possible, it has the result that each kick is more powerful, more precise and quicker. It also means that the attacker can kick low or high, depending on their opponent.

These wide-ranging stretching exercises were always done in pairs and the instructor would choose the pairs for us. One of the exercises which was executed, was when one of the pair would raise their leg on to the other's shoulder and a minute later change legs and shoulders accordingly, after which they swapped around. We were encouraged to move our head to our leg and touch our toes with the opposite hand. This extra part of the stretch, further enhanced every move we would subsequently rehearse, in the next stage of the lesson.

Another stretching exercise, would have both partners standing back to back and one would bend their knees, until their back was in line with the bottom of their partner's back. With a slow movement, the partner would be carefully lifted on to the back of the other and if this was done properly, with balance and accuracy, the partner could simply just lie on their opponent's back whilst they felt their muscles being stretched. I remember how I could always feel my back distending and indeed, hear the click...click of other backs around the room stretching.

One of the stretching exercises I personally found the most challenging, was when my partner and I would sit on the floor, opposite each other. One of us would have our legs spread apart, as wide as we could possibly go and the other would use his or her legs to gently push their partner's legs further apart, by placing their feet just below the knee and slowly pushing. It would obviously depend on the flexibility of the individual, as to how far their legs could be pushed. Those who were really flexible could have their legs pushed right out, until they were in line with each other (like doing the splits). I was one of these people, so the extra challenge for me, was to then, whilst in the 'splits' position, move my torso forward and have my head and chest touching the floor. It was only after a couple of years of training, that I was able to do this.

Nonetheless, I found this particular exercise to be the most difficult, because of the pain barrier I had to go through. Stretching my legs was fairly easy, having them pushed that bit further was a bit more challenging and attempting to get my head and chest to the floor was even more of an effort. But to top it all off, one of my most experienced instructors would slowly walk up behind me and push my back. I could always see him approaching and I always braced myself for what I knew was to come. He would place his left hand on the small of my back, with his right hand on the top of my back, between my shoulder blades and push, slowly but deliberately. I always heard him say, 'Deep breaths, Nic, deep breaths,' and that's exactly what I would do, as the pain intensified and remained, like a lingering sensation of discomfort, which lasted for only a minute, but seemed like an eternity.

My instructor would then slowly release the pressure on my back and I would very gradually bring my head and torso into the upright position. Although the pain was over for another week, this 'procedure' would always leave me with a sensation of achievement and accomplishment and made me feel empowered to use my legs, as well as my hands and fists, to attack a sparring partner and defend myself. I would often relate to others, how these stretching exercises made me feel a bit like a rubber band, being pulled and stretched, this way and that.

But the flexibility it gave me was incredible and the pain barrier I fought through regularly, made having that extra suppleness even more worthwhile.

Every time I walked away from the radiotherapy treatment room, I would be filled with those same feelings of achievement and accomplishment. I had been waiting to be called for my daily dose of radiation and then I was accompanied into the treatment room. I lay down on the table, the mask was fixed into place and the treatment began. I looked carefully at the 'lead pencil', which seemed to be hovering above me and I could almost taste the nauseous smells of ozone, mixed in with the more pleasant smell of oil of cloves. Each and every time on that radiotherapy table was demanding, but as the radiographers came in to unscrew the mask and help me to sit up after each treatment, I felt a sense of empowerment. Just like those agile legs of mine had given me a sense of achievement, so too, did each radiotherapy session leave me feeling empowered (as well as, of course, tired and feeling terribly sore), in my fight to shrink the tumour and fry it in to oblivion.

Samson's Fight with a Lion

The famous story from the Book of Judges, tells how Samson, a biblical character with immense physical strength, struggled and overcame an attack by a lion. Samson tore the lion apart with his bare hands and later on, he revisited the spot where the lion lay dead and noticed that a swarm of bees had formed a hive within the carcass. Samson declared, 'From the eater came forth food and from the strong came forth sweetness.' (Judges Chp. 14)

Just as Samson fought with and overcame the ferocity of the lion, so too, many people have fought with and overcome cancers. But to take the comparison a step further, in relation to this biblical episode; my sweetness is the clear realisation that life is so very fragile. I could be here today and gone tomorrow. Yes, I live with a degree of fear, but I learn to temper that fear, to control it - to use it to my advantage. I let it tell me, that the fight is worth it and I am on my guard when I must be.

But it is the moments of silence, thought and pensiveness that allow feelings to gather and at that moment, I must stay strong, bold and not allow those feelings to go astray. Keep strong.

We don't know when our time to move on from this world will come, but we must fight with all our human might and know one thing; the superpower I call God, I believe, sees the bigger picture and He does know how our whole life will pan out. Samson was only blessed with supernatural strength, because that is what God wanted. Similarly, however much effort I put in, whatever ammunition I use, whichever strategy I prefer, in the end we will all come face to face with our destiny, be it clearly good or seemingly bad. If it seems bad, don't let this dampen the fight, but keep focused. Knowing that there is a fight worth winning, I believe, is the sweetness, because not to know that a fight is there for the taking, is unthinkable to me.

For me to say that life, post-cancer is, in general, sweet, would probably sound a little far-fetched to say the least and at most, a bit extreme. It is sweet, because whatever comes a person's way, they always have the experience of fighting cancer to fall back on and this fight makes most other fights seem trivial. After all, what is more valuable than life itself? Nevertheless, those nearest and dearest to me have had to remind me of this from time to time and once they remind me of the enormity of what I have been through, of all I have experienced in my fight with cancer, I begin to put everything in to perspective.

It is certainly not the case that the fight against cancer simply trivialises all other fights because it doesn't. But, it allows me to think and weigh up the enormity, or otherwise, of each situation and each potential fight. It enables me to ask, 'Is this really a fight, or can I find another way to get out of this problematic situation?' The answer is usually the latter – there's another way - and if that is the case (compared to fighting cancer which is not a definite win situation), then that potential fight becomes more of a scuffle or small hurdle that I have to climb over. But climb over I shall and all will be well. When faced with a day to day problem, there is usually a solution, with a number of strategies available, all of which can bring about a definite resolution. On the other hand, when faced with a cancer, an enigma and illusive disease, one does not know for certain that the strategies at their disposal, whether conventional or otherwise, will suffice and help them overcome this enemy. So the experience of cancer certainly does help people to differentiate the real fights from the mere hurdles.

When a boxer steps into the ring, however much preparation he has done, however much time has been spent with sparring partners, he still won't know for certain the outcome of the fight. He will have probably trained himself to think positively, to visualise a victory and a path to which that victory will transpire, but he still won't know for sure. This is the cruelty of cancer and the nature of this disease. This hidden enemy requires a certain amount of faith, hope and belief, that it can be overcome. After all, to lose the fight is so final. All this is very different to most other fights, for here the end result is usually not so clear and it is the doubt of what the prognosis will definitely be, which makes this fight against cancer one of the toughest of all.

I remember going to the hospital for a check-up about three years ago and I casually pointed out another lump in my nose to the consultant surgeon. I was almost sure that he would tell me not to worry, as he usually did (I am a bit of a worrier, but understandably so – I think), but this time he told me he was worried and concerned as to what that lump might be. I immediately thought to myself, 'Never take things for granted.' I am duly reminded of Mike Tyson's fight with Buster Douglas. It was meant to be just another victory for Tyson, but Douglas caught him out and I felt a little caught out by the sudden look of concern on the surgeon's face. I asked him if he was sure about it, to which he replied affirmatively. 'So, what next?' I asked myself. Not again, I thought. How could it be? I thought. But…but…

My wife was with me at the time and a good job she was, because of the sanity she instils in me all the time and the correct perspective she has in these kinds of situations. The consultant surgeon explained to us, that there is always a small risk of the radiation from the radiotherapy causing problems later in life and this was his fear. So, I underwent another biopsy and another week of waiting for the results and I immediately sprung in to action, much like a boxer upon hearing the 'seconds out' and the bell. I knew exactly what I needed to do, after all, I had been here before and was 'experienced' at this. I pictured myself talking to myself, giving strong words of advice. But nothing I had undergone was quite like this experience.

I was told by the surgeons that a general anaesthetic would not be necessary, as it was a matter of simply cutting a small piece of the lump from the inside of my nose. It all sounded quite straight forward. The day came and I waited…and waited…and waited. Finally, I was called and accompanied down to the operating theatre. Once inside, I lay on a table and from above, a very powerful light shone down on my face, a bit like looking directly at the sun. In fact, even when I told one of the many people around me, that the light was ever so bright, the towel they put over my eyes still didn't completely remove the immense brightness of that light.

Never mind, I thought to myself and lay with my eyes closed. 'I am going to spray some local anaesthetic up your nose,' said the surgeon. That's good, I thought, it will certainly dull the pain. The surgeon sprayed a bit of the liquid and as he did so, I felt myself heave, desperately trying to catch my breath and tell the surgeons of the discomfort I was going through, as a result of the liquid being sprayed up my nose. You see, when you have a large cavity in your face, any water seems to go straight down your throat without warning. As I eventually caught my breath, I informed the surgeon of the discomfort and he duly set my mind at rest by explaining what he was about to do. I think he did the right thing, to just move on with the procedure. After all, the area was now numb and there wasn't going to be any need for more anaesthetic.

I'm not sure whether it's better being awake for these sorts of procedures, or asleep. At least, if you are asleep, you have no need to worry, to process explanations being given to you. You just lie back and stay out of it, so to speak. But being fully awake, I could speak to the surgeon and I did just that. 'What if it is cancer?' I asked. 'How can you get rid of it?' The surgeon replied, 'Well, I am good at rebuilding noses...' I felt like time had quickly rewound at a rate of years, thirteen to be precise and I was being told I had cancer and preparing for the incumbent fight. What was I to do now? I thought. I lay there cold, shocked and purposely silent. They wheeled me into the recovery room, despite me being fully awake and completely aware of my surroundings and I lay there worrying. 'Fighting spirit,' I thought, but perhaps there was nothing to fight for. Perhaps it wasn't cancer; it was just the not knowing that made me tense.

My wife and I took a taxi home and we arrived late at night. We spoke to my parents about what the surgeon had said and all the possible eventualities.

Once I had overcome the initial shock, I felt myself back in fighting mode. When I was partnered to spar against an opponent who looked bigger, stronger and more skilful than me, I would be a bag of nerves, until the moment I started the two minute spar. At that point I was well-away, thinking and negotiating my next move to overcome my opponent. So too, with this unknown entity. Now that I was in the midst of a fight, to get through the next few days with a positive and hopeful mindset, I was able to tap into all the resources that I had come to know over the past thirteen years. So I fought through that week, always remaining positive and always telling myself that whatever the results of the biopsy, I would use the 'fighting spirit' I had come to know so well.

A few days later my wife and I caught the Tube and travelled into London and to the hospital outpatients department to get the results. I suppose you would expect my heart to be racing, but it wasn't. I had made plans in my mind, but first and foremost, my strategy was to remain positive, to think only good! What happened next was almost surreal. The registrar called my wife and I into his office and he proceeded to examine me, looking up my nose and into the cavity in my mouth. 'We've come here for some important results,' we said, almost in unison. The registrar didn't really seem too bothered and proceeded to talk to me about how to keep the inside of my nose moist! Truly unreal!

We thanked the surgeon very much for his time and as we exited his office we, almost literally, bumped into the consultant surgeon. The one who had done the biopsy. The one who I had come to trust and the one whom I had hoped I would be seeing that morning. 'Everything is OK, Nicky. The biopsy showed that it was simply some hard tissue in your nose which formed the lump.' I think that is what he said, but it didn't matter. All I could hear was 'it isn't cancer' and I was overjoyed, as too were my family and friends.

A fighter still has to spar and train from time to time, to keep in practise and not lose that cutting edge. Perhaps this was my practise spar? I guess I'll never know, but it certainly keeps me on my toes.

The Battle with Food...and Drink

I suppose the first time that I actually realised my disadvantages with eating and drinking was shortly after I left hospital following the Maxillectomy (the big operation to remove the cancer from my face) and I caught the Tube to go back for a check-up. I had just drunk a bottle of orange juice, the contents of which, I realised only later and to my horror, were flowing out of my nose. I didn't realise at all, because many of the nerves in the right-hand side of my face had been severed during the successful operation. I approached the ticket office (before the days of Oyster cards) and the guard said to me 'You need to wipe your nose sir.' I was so embarrassed and quickly thrust a tissue from my pocket to my nose.

Just picture the scene: a large table full of food and drink, from smoked salmon sandwiches and bagels filled with a variety of spreads, to freshly squeezed orange juice, lemonade and cola. Then there's the human company; work colleagues, associates and other dignitaries, are all milling around the hall, plates filled with delicacies and glasses of drink in hand. It all looks so appealing, but I daren't take any food or drink, for fear of being caught out, of being made to look bad. So, I tell myself, 'Use the fighting spirit, use the fighting spirit!'

A combination of radiotherapy and surgery have left my mouth-opening severely restricted, to the extent that a delicacy for me, includes (what they call in the medical profession) 'slops'. Some would gaze longingly at a portion of steak and chips, or lick their lips as they are about to bite in to a cheeseburger or hamburger. Yet my palate is wet by the sight of a bowl of Weetabix that has been standing in milk for five minutes; by cottage cheese and avocado paste; by soups of all kinds. I have become accustomed to these foods because they are so easy to eat, without making a mess around my mouth and on the plate in front of me. As for the drink, I have to be so careful not to take too much liquid, for fear of choking or the contents of the mouthful coming through my nose. It used to be so embarrassing and I simply wouldn't eat or drink in public, until I became determined to overcome this fear and overcome it I did, with the 'fighting spirit'.

I have subsequently developed a procedure for eating and drinking. I am careful to keep my head upright, to only take small mouthfuls, to eat small amounts at a time and to prepare myself for the time when, yes, some drink may come out my nose or some food might be stuck on my upper lip. It happens to the best of us! Only when I have explained the reason it happens to me, to the person with whom I am conversing, they become absorbed in the story I proceed to tell them (I tell them the shortened version!).

To some, it wouldn't seem like much of a 'fight' to simply eat or drink something, but for me it really is an effort, especially in public. But, if one is determined and I certainly am, to speak to colleagues and dignitaries about topics and subjects which will enhance my knowledge and understanding of my profession, to have the opportunity to further my career, then I will muster the strength (as would a fighter) to push myself forward.

A fighter, preparing for a fight, has to push himself, through feelings of tiredness and feelings of being unmotivated. They must drive themselves through these negative feelings if they are to triumph. I will not acquire the knowledge and skills learnt from my peers, if I do not push myself through difficult circumstances and as trivial as it may sound, eating and drinking in public is a challenging circumstance I am determined to fight through.

I am, once again, reminded of one of the martial arts classes I used to attend. How there was always a regular nucleus of people who would attend the class week-in and week-out, much like myself. Sparring with these people, you knew what to expect, you knew their styles. You became used to their strong points and their weak points. But then, there was the guy or girl who would show up one week, who had never been to the class before. You knew, by the colour of their belt, how wary of them you had to be. To spar with them was not so easy and you had to be on your guard, vigilant, cautious of their every move.

Once I had been diagnosed with cancer and a treatment plan put in place, I definitely knew what I was up against, but this made the fight no less difficult. I knew the strategies and 'moves' which I would use (the doctors and surgeons had explained them to me) and I recognised what had to be done.

In contrast, waking up with half my mouth gone, with no teeth on the upper right-hand side of my mouth, part of my hard palate removed, no bone and a gaping cavity, I was in a bewildered state, confused by the absolute unknown. Of course the surgeons had explained the procedure to me beforehand, but there is nothing like the real thing! This was truly like an occasion where, years before, an unknown person had walked in to the martial arts class and I had to spar with them, to try to determine their next move. To work out how to eat, drink and speak was a difficult undertaking and one which would take quite a bit of emotional strength.

Of course, the emotional strength comes from within every person, but there are those friends and family, not to mention the nurses, doctors, surgeons and other health workers, who help to build up an emotional fortification and a strong will and determination to succeed. I don't believe the fight can be fought, let alone won, without them. Even Mike Tyson, who became the youngest boxer to win the WBC, WBA and IBF World Heavyweight titles at 20 years, 4 months and 22 days of age, only got where he did because of his support. Listening to a recording of Tyson talking about his first trainer, Cus D'Amato, he explains how D'Amato gave him the self-conviction and belief to become the champion of the world. You would think that a tough guy like Tyson wasn't afraid, but (as he explains) he too was afraid before his first fight and his trainer gave him the confidence to triumph again and again and again.

To prepare to fight against an opponent such as cancer, you also need support. Members of the family who continuously call, visit, run errands. The friends who organise rotas to and from the hospital, cook meals, come to visit or simply leave a message or write a note to say that they care and you are in their thoughts and prayers all the time. The people who leave anonymous envelopes with hundreds of pounds in them, because they know you have gone down to half pay at work, yet still have a family to feed. These are the 'corner-men', the Cus D'Amato equivalents, who instil a belief and a drive to want to succeed come what may. I was in the extremely fortunate position to have the most caring team of health professionals one could ask for. The oncologists always explained everything, from the procedures of radiotherapy, to the rigours of chemotherapy. When the loneliness got the better of me or when an injection of positivity was needed, the nurses, doctors and surgeons were there and each and every surgical procedure was explained and questions answered in their entirety. This was my 'corner', my support, my confidence boost and my self-belief. It was the care and support of family, friends and health workers who made me feel like I was heavyweight champion of the world.

Nothing Short of a Miracle

The unknown foreign body in my mouth, following the operation to remove the cancer, was (as I mentioned earlier) at first seen as a menace. But how wrong I was and time, together with experience, has proven this to me. At first glance, the mouth-piece looks fairly simple, comprising of a sheet of metal fitted precisely to the contours, curves and shape of my mouth, gums and teeth. Then the teeth were moulded on to the metal, together with a gum-coloured material, to replace the gums and teeth that had to be removed. Perhaps the most important parts of my mouth-piece are the clips, which fix on to my existing natural teeth and keep the whole mouth-piece in place. As well as the need to make the prosthesis look similar to one's real teeth, there is also the necessity to make it practical and enable eating, drinking and speaking. No, I'm not an excessive talker, in fact quite the contrary, as I prefer to sit and listen and only then make a contribution where it is necessary. But in my profession of teaching, speaking is a requirement and a necessity; speaking to colleagues, to parents and to children with intelligibility, intonation and clarity is very important.

As I was cleaning my teeth and cavity one summer's day in August, I took out the prosthesis and to my utter horror one of the clips broke clean off in my hand. Until that moment, I suppose I took this ever so important section of my mouth for granted. If someone had been standing in the bathroom there and then with a video camera, they would have seen my face turn white and my eyes widen in absolute disbelief. They would have filmed me standing by the bathroom sink, holding the broken clip in my right hand and the rest of the prosthesis in my left hand, with my eyes looking at the clip and then at the mouth-piece. Clip to mouth-piece, clip to mouth-piece, over and over again. It seemed an eternity, but was probably no more than three minutes, before I pulled myself together, placed the prosthesis back in my mouth (as best I could) and went downstairs to make a phone call. The ever so supportive and helpful prosthodontist at the hospital, immediately phoned the laboratory which made these devices and within half an hour, I was on a train to the lab.

As I sat on the train, with the mouth-piece loose in my mouth, I thought of the potential problems this could cause me. In this case I was fortunate, as it was the summer holidays from school and therefore there were obviously no teachers, colleagues, parents or children to talk to. I had also just had breakfast (my usual slops and a cup of coffee) and therefore wasn't thinking about eating at the present time. But how would I eat and drink with a broken prosthesis? The well-known saying

'You don't appreciate something, until you no longer have it', sprung to mind and I felt a sense of helplessness and vulnerability.

I hurriedly walked along the street and turned into the entrance of the lab, where a friendly face asked me to show him the problem. I cautiously unwrapped a tissue, to reveal the broken metal clip. I then proceeded to remove the rest of the prosthesis from my mouth and the technician studied it, turning it this way and that, assuring me that it would be fixed in approximately 45 minutes. I nodded at him, lest my Darth-Vader, muffled-like tones, which were hardly audible, didn't send the intended message of 'that's fine and I am so very grateful. Please just fix it as soon as you can.' (The absence of the hard palate makes words difficult to hear, as there is a flow of air between the mouth and nose.)

I sat there in the waiting room, sort of hoping that no one else would come into the lab and hoping whole-heartedly that no one would ask me anything, to which I would feel compelled to reply. This is the miracle of technology, the miracle of science, so much of which we take for granted and although it would be difficult to speak, eat and drink, I suppose there is always a way out of every situation. A fighter caught on the ropes, backed into a corner, with seemingly no way out of the situation, has to think and work out a strategy, a tactic that will release him from this apparently no-way-out situation and enable him to continue the fight. Once again, the kindness and willingness of these health professionals had reminded me that for every situation there is a solution. Whenever I have run into these types of difficulties, there has always been someone who will willingly and through sheer kindness, make it their business to sort out my problem. I am eternally grateful to these noble people.

The Maccabees, David and Those Who Help Themselves

In the Book of Maccabees I and II, it describes how in the year 167 BCE, Judah Maccabeus, son of Mattathias Hasmon, led a twenty five -year struggle, in which he challenged and was victorious over, the Assyrian Greeks. The Maccabees were severely outnumbered during their battle, but the superpower of the day were defeated and forced to relinquish their hold on the Jewish Temple, standing in all its glory, in Jerusalem.

Whilst the Maccabees, a group of organised fighters, declared their belief in the God of the Israelites and understood that without His divine guidance, they would not be victorious, they also believed in helping themselves. This belief in self-help is highlighted in a much earlier episode, when, as the Children of Israel were trapped between the Red Sea and the fast approaching Egyptian army, a small number of them jumped into the water, as this was the only course of action that would have any chance of keeping them alive. It was after this courageous act, that the Bible relates how the waters of the Red Sea miraculously parted and the people walked across to the other side and to safety.

The Maccabees didn't sit around waiting for a miracle to occur, but took up arms and did whatever they could to defeat their enemy. They believed that it was through this self-determination, that they wouldn't easily relinquish their land; together with the belief, that once their actions were recognised by God, He would intervene and make them victorious.

The first time I faced my very own encounter with the might of the carcinoma (cancer) in my face, I was quite simply shocked. I remember it well, as I stood there in my parents' hallway, a bit like a rabbit in the head lights, thinking and praying. But with the inner belief that I had the ability to help myself, as well as pray and ask for help from a Higher Force, it made me emotionally stronger. I would use everything at my disposal, to rid myself of this slimy antagonist.

Indeed, another famous biblical story, which took place many years before that of the Maccabees, was the story of the shepherd boy David (before he became king) and Goliath. The story relates, that the Israelites see this huge Philistine, giant of a man, clad in a copper helmet, wearing armour of chain mail, a copper shield on his legs and a copper neck-guard between his shoulders. The Bible relates how Goliath's spear was like a weaver's beam and the blade of his spear was huge, making the Israelites flee for their lives and the young, shepherd boy

David witnesses their fear. Goliath then challenges the Israelite army and says, 'Choose yourselves a man and let him come down to me. If he can fight me and kill me, we will be slaves to you. If I defeat him and kill him, you will be slaves to us and serve us.' Upon hearing this, the people were petrified.

Eventually, David steps forward, unperturbed by this huge figure of a giant and recalls the number of times, whilst watching his father's flock, he had to fend off attacks from bears and lions. He declares his unmoving faith in Almighty God and runs toward the Philistine giant, Goliath, who mocks David for barely being armed with any weapons (David had explained to King Saul that as he was only a young lad, the weapons were far too heavy for him). Whilst running toward the enemy, David puts his hand into a bag and pulls out a small rock, places it in to his sling and directs it at Goliath's head. It strikes him, cleanly on the temple and he falls to the ground, dead. Once the Philistine army, watching from a distance, witnesses this completely unorthodox defeat of their hero, they flee.

When I read the story of David and Goliath, it is obviously amazing how a young lad like David, with comparatively no battle experience, has the bravery and the fortitude to face this titanic figure of a giant. David doesn't refuse to take the weapons he is offered because he feels he doesn't need them. He doesn't take the weapons, because they are simply too heavy for him. So, he takes the one weapon at his disposal and which is the most effective; his slingshot and uses it to the greatest effect.

Whilst elusive and cunning, the tumour in my head and neck was my Goliath and it had to be defeated. Unlike David, I was most certainly scared; terrified of what the future would bring, fearful of the prognosis, frightened at the prospect of eating, drinking, having to wear a mouth-piece. But, like David, I used the weapons at my disposal, every tool in my armoury to fight with determination and every sinew in my body and mind, to walk boldly up to this aggressor and strike it, not just once, but again and again and again. I would do everything in my power, not to become a slave to cancer and its after-effects.

To Overpower a Brick

As I look at a photograph of myself on the mantelpiece at home, standing over two halves of a brick, I am reminded of one of the many tasks I had to accomplish when attempting to earn my black belt. Amongst a number of tasks, I had to literally 'chop' a brick in half and although I had seen it done many times in films and also in real life, to have to do this myself, seemed somewhat impossible.

I started to practise with a large money bag, which was given to me by Steven, made of a soft material and filled with sand. It was sown together quite tightly at the corners and I used this regularly, to apply the 'chopping' technique which one of my instructors and good friend Steven had shown me.

I would lay the money bag on the floor and position my left foot on the left hand side, next to the bag. My right foot was about half a metre behind and I used it to give leverage to the power which was to come through my arm and hand and down on to the bag. Then, I would position my right hand straight, with all fingers out and rigid and my thumb tucked in slightly, behind the palm of my hand. The actual strike came from the side of the hand next to the little finger, with the palm very slightly facing inwards.

I would raise my hand high, before going through the motions of coming down on to the bag, but stopping an inch away from it. I would do this again and again, until I felt psychologically ready to actually strike the bag. When my hand eventually did make contact with the sand-filled bag, the impact was hardly remarkable, after all, it was only a sand-bag! I practised this procedure over and over again, but never with a brick, until the day itself.

When the moment finally arrived for me to chop the brick, as part of my black belt grading, my name was called and I walked up to the brick. Both ends of the brick lay on two other bricks either side and underneath there was a large paving slab. I had trained hard for this moment and I focused my mind completely on the job at hand, the two key words firmly etched on my mind, 'fighting spirit'. I looked at the brick with a focus and concentration, the likes that one would apply to an epic scene in an enticing film or book and I positioned myself accordingly. I told myself that I simply had to break the brick. That the force and power I would send through it, would be so great that it would actually break the slab underneath the brick. I told this to myself each time I raised my arm. Hand, fingers, palm at the ready, 'fighting spirit'. I went through the motions over and over again, my breathing becoming increasingly heavier, as I psyched myself up. When my mind and breathing had reached a crescendo, BANG....my hand, together with the full weight of my body came down on to the brick and it broke in two.

When I knew that I had to face the battle with cancer, I applied the same rules, except this time, I was given no time to train. No time to get used to the motion of coming down on to it with a force and breaking it in two. No time to emotionally prepare myself for the pain and the feeling of helplessness. But I did have training and a resolve, the 'fighting spirit', which I would apply as best I could. The preparation to actually breaking the brick was a focal point in my fight with this obscure form, which had developed in my face and I would use the same mind-set to prepare to 'break' the cancer.

The breaking of this illusive enemy, was the successful operation to remove it from my head and later, my neck. But, to do this would need preparation and the radio and chemotherapy, together with the months of visualisation and positivity, would be the modes of weakening my unwanted adversary.

I focused on the cancer and with each comparable deep breath and dedicated determination, I went through the motions of ridding this cancer from my face, of preparing myself. Until the final blow, when the first motion, with my psyche set and my mind focused: radiotherapy; the second motion: chemotherapy; the third motion: visualisation, now becoming even more psyched-up and determined and then the BLOW: the Maxillectomy. The mass of cancerous cells is in no way, as rock-hard as a brick, but as anyone who has shared my experiences will testify, 'Give me a brick to break any day!'

Vaccination to Add to the Fortification

In the vast majority of sports, especially the contact sports (perhaps Australian rules football being the exception!) there are different forms of protective gear which can be worn by the participants. This enables the sportsmen and women to be at their very best, while also being protected. It is because of this protection, that the sport is usually played with full vigour by both parties. Take both regular hockey and ice hockey as an example; those hockey sticks can be vicious if waved in the face of an opponent and therefore a mouthguard is worn. Similarly, footballers wear shin pads, boxers wear different weighted gloves, depending on the fighter's own weight (or indeed head guards in amateur boxing), Formula 1 racing drivers wear helmets and fire resistant clothing and jockeys wear helmets. I could go on and on, but the point is, that each sport has protective gear that enables the maximum participation.

In a similar vein, as a primary school teacher who has taken children on many outward bound adventure weeks away, I know of the need for all children and staff to be vaccinated against things like tetanus. Once the doctor or nurse has given the simple, but effective vaccine, one can usually fully take part in climbing trees, crawling through mud and swinging from 20-foot zip wires.

As I recovered from a year of radiotherapy, chemotherapy, operations, wearing of prosthetics and more, I was fortunate to be introduced to a professor of oncology at another London hospital. I say that I was fortunate, because he was currently in the midst of trialling a vaccine against different types of cancers and I was even more fortunate to get an appointment with him.

The vaccine being trialled was very similar to the BCG vaccine we all used to get given when we were about 13 to 15-years-old, against tuberculosis. I remember that well, because of the swelling it produced a few days after the injection. I vividly recall all the pupils in my year showing off their blisters, competing with each other as to whose was the most sore. I even remember how guys would go up to each other and hit them on the arm as a joke (although hardly a joke for the recipient).

Well, this vaccine did just the same, as it left me with a swelling and a sore; the patterns of scars at the top of my left arm, which serve as a reminder that I once had a series of these injections, about 25 in total. I hasten to add, that the patients certainly did NOT go around displaying their scars to all! I was given these injections every three months to begin with and then every six months. I also felt extremely lucky, as an oncologist would always give me a thorough health check before they administered the vaccine.

At the same time as being given these injections, the professor also told me about the anti-oxidant effects of green tea, fruit and vegetables and vitamins A, C, E and selenium. (I hasten to add, that green tea in its pure form, is certainly an acquired taste, but I was told by the medical professionals that it is more effective than the green tea blends which can be bought!) As I understood it, the human body produces rogue cells called 'free-radicals' which can turn in to cancers and it's things like fruit, vegetables, green tea and a variety of healthy vitamins which can help the body produce 'antioxidants', which keep these free-radicals at bay, thus preventing them from turning in to nasty things, such as cancers.

Following my conversation with the professor, regarding the different types of foods and nutrients that could protect me and the series of regular vaccinations I was due to receive, for what amounted to a period of about five years (until the funding came to an end!), I felt a kind of reassurance, the likes of which I hadn't had until now. I felt that suddenly I had a kind of protection, a safeguard and fortification which would help me through life. Just like a footballer who doesn't usually purposely stamp on an opponent's leg with the intention of breaking it, or a jockey who doesn't purposely fly off his horse head first, or a racing driver who doesn't intentionally drive his car or bike into a wall, I was always going to try to lead as healthy a life as I could. (I would like to emphasise, that I had never drank alcohol and a cigarette had and never has, touched my lips.) I was never going to take things for granted again and I was going to be forever vigilant for changes to my body - lumps and bumps, etc. But I had a kind of defence, in the form of the vaccine and the different vitamins I was being recommended by a doctor of conventional medicine.

Unfortunately, some five years after the vaccine had first been given to me, the professor kindly telephoned me, to explain that the trial was coming to an end due to a lack of funds. I was obviously quite taken aback by this sudden and unexpected news, but I once again, raised my eyes to the heavens (as one so often sees footballers doing, upon scoring a goal) and voiced my eternal gratitude.

Discipline is the Key to the Fight

The need to be disciplined when training for a fight and all it involves, is analogous with the comparative fight with cancer.

Anyone who has sparred with someone, for just two minutes, will tell you of the immense exhaustion and fatigue which hits them. So to fight for at least ten, three minute rounds, as professional boxers do, requires a fitness level of epic proportions. Not only does a fighter have to keep moving and focused, but they also have to exert an enormous amount of energy when they unleash a blow to their opponent, whether it is a kick or a punch.

This fitness level comes from a determination to train hard, which is driven by an incomparable discipline, which in turn, ensures the fighter is 'up to scratch', fit, supple and strong. The early morning runs, the late night swims, the carefully controlled diet, the unsociable hours of training. All these contribute to a successful fighter, who will be a match for any opponent.

When I was training for the black belt, I underwent a rigorous regime of training. Firstly, I would attend four martial arts evening classes each week, run four miles a day (which included a circuit training course on the route of the run), swim twice a week and train one-to-one with friends. I suppose I became a bit obsessed with the training, especially the need to get in as many practise sparring sessions as possible and also the circuit training, which I would compulsively ensure I did properly, or I would do it all again! The early morning runs, long and inconvenient train rides to and from classes and the one-to-one fighting sessions with friends, were demanding and challenged one's inner core.

But, so too were the early morning trips to the hospital for radiotherapy, the hours of waiting, as the chemotherapy drug attached to my arm via a drip, slowly filtered in to my vein and the discipline which was required, when being told that I had to wait for a conclusive medical opinion. Perhaps, the most discipline was required for the concoction of drugs I had to take; some during the day, but some late at night and in the early hours of the morning.

Try to imagine; there were times I was in so much pain that I couldn't keep still, I couldn't sleep. I was constantly restless and the only pain relief was carefully prescribed and monitored Morphine. But then the other drugs had to be taken (anti-sickness and other pain relief tablets) and no sooner had I found some solace and fallen asleep, when I was being awoken by those who cared very much, to take a new batch of medicines.

I could quite easily have rolled over and ignored the pleas to take these medicines, but I knew instinctively, that they were going to help get rid of this annoying fiend inside my body. The above scenario seemed to go on for an eternity, but I remained disciplined in my fight.

Similarly, the long hours of waiting and days of hospitalisation for chemotherapy, the daily trips to the hospital for blood tests and radiotherapy and the lonely, sometimes despairing, hours as an inpatient, when I had no visitors and the world seemed a very solitary place. All these moments required an acute discipline, the likes of which were built in to my easy-going, patient and calm nature and which I had become accustomed to, years earlier, during my training experiences.

Even when the obturator, the mouth prosthesis, was put into my mouth, replacing half my hard palate and teeth, despite the initial depression, I knew I had to remain disciplined. I had to eat, despite not wanting to, as it was difficult. I had to drink, despite the contents of the bottle or cup running out my nose. I had to speak, despite my confidence being at rock-bottom. I had to rally and I had to march on, regardless of the hurdles I had to face at every juncture.

As I continue marching on through life's ups and downs, I still have the patience and self-control which are needed to keep me disciplined. Life never stops putting hurdles in our way and it never stops testing us, with an on-going need to fight back.

Nevertheless, it is the discipline which is the key to the fight.

Another Fighter in My Life

As my brother strolled along the pavement on a warm and pleasant summer's day, on the way to the local shops, a poster on a tree caught his eye. It wasn't the usual poster one sometimes sees pinned to a tree, requesting the public to keep their eyes peeled for a lost cat or dog. In place of a photograph of a missing pet, there was the image of a man with a muscular, powerful, martial art-type build. The piece of paper which hung from the tree, affixed by two drawing pins read, 'Martial Arts/Self-Defence Trainer available to teach all ages, for a one-to-one weekly training session.' My brother almost walked straight past it, thinking it was indeed another plea for the return of someone's missing feline friend. However, when the words 'Self-Defence' and 'Trainer' caught his eye, he did a double take. He had trained in martial arts as a teenager and lifted weights and was keen for his own children, now teenagers themselves, to get started with some kind of fitness regime and self-defence. He took out his mobile phone and punched in the number which appeared at the foot of the poster, carefully saving it in his contacts for later that day.

That evening, he scrolled down his contacts and called and spoke to the gentleman who had used the tree to advertise and share his self-defence expertise. Gabriel introduced himself to my brother and they booked a first training session for early the following week.

Over the next few weeks, that one training session grew to about 15 different weekly training sessions with different people, as one friend after another, one relative after another, got word of this gentle, but formidable giant. He not only had the proficiency in a variety of fighting and self-defence techniques, but also had the aptitude for teaching others, to boost their confidence and to stand up and defend themselves, if and when necessary.

As a result of the various procedures which had been performed on my face, I have always been conscious of the need to take great care in protecting it. For example, when walking across the playground in the school at which I work, I am always fully alert to the flying footballs and tennis balls, which come at me from every direction, although I can assure you it is not intentional! For this reason, I had not felt comfortable when training in self-defence (or any contact/semi-contact activity) with others, even those of my own standard. I was really looking to find someone who was an exceptionally skilful martial artist, who would be able to throw a punch or a kick directed to my face, but be able to pull it short, or 'just miss'! That 'someone' was Gabriel and I acquainted myself with him as we set up a weekly training session.

Of course, during my first session with Gabriel, I was cautious and continually worried about my face being hurt. I hesitated as the thought kept re-entering my mind, 'Was this a good idea? Perhaps martial arts is not really for me anymore!' I contemplated the reality of a blow to the face; my obturator twisted and damaged, the bones under my eye socket disfigured, my nose broken or my remaining natural teeth knocked out. All these thoughts rushed through my mind and I felt a sense of negligence. How could I be so careless as to train in a contact sport, which may well result in a potentially significant injury to my face?

Having trained in martial arts for a good few years, I knew how to recognise an expert in the field. I could easily tell that the accuracy of all of Gabriel's moves, including his punches and kicks, were absolutely precise. So despite these feelings of doubt regarding my face, the trust I had in Gabriel was the overriding factor in the new-found confidence which I had now discovered.

Here was someone with whom, at last, I could comfortably train. Gabriel made sure to tell me, 'I won't hurt you Nic, but I will push you to your limits and beyond.' This was exactly what I had wanted and now I had a trainer, a confidante who could get the very best out of me and train me to my maximum.

We trained, week in and week out and I slowly, but very surely, felt the skills I had once excelled at, return. This was all thanks to Gabriel, who had been the instrument in re-igniting that fighting flame.

You Have to Use That Second Wind

When Gabriel informed me he would still push me to my limit, despite my disabilities and facial intricacies, I didn't quite understand the enormity of this statement. After all, I had been training using an exercise bike and running in the streets, for the duration of my absence from martial arts. I also added some push-ups and stomach exercises to my training schedule. As a result of my commitment to using the exercise bike and keeping in shape with sit-ups, crunches and a whole host of stomach exercises, as well as push ups, I felt fit and ready to train with Gabriel. However, this training which I was about to embark on, was like no other I had experienced in recent years. Nevertheless, this exercise regime was the key to my growing confidence in a variety of areas of my life, not just self-defence and martial arts.

One of Gabriel's favourite phrases, which he used on many an occasion, particularly when free-sparring, was '…Nic, use your second wind…' At first I wasn't sure exactly what he meant, but I soon understood that this statement applied to the environment in which I found myself. It meant that when Gabriel and I were sparring (full contact, minus my head!) and the feeling of absolute exhaustion started to prevail, it was at that point that I was to take stock, take a number of deep breaths and continue to fight with a renewed vigour, a new drive. At first, I would ask Gabriel how to muster that new energy and how to suddenly (when needed) invoke an inner surge of vitality, which would enable me to keep fighting with aggression, yet precision.

At the end of one of my first few sessions with Gabriel, he explained where the 'second wind' comes from. He told me that it could be found in the core of a person (as he pointed to the middle of his torso), a place from which the energy flows, a place which lends itself to the vigour which must be found, when all seems hopeless and lost.

I can imagine that there are indeed, lots of different sports which firmly encourage the use of a second wind, be it athletics, football, tennis, cricket or rugby, to name but a few. If the sportsman or woman is giving 100 per cent of their energy and commitment to the cause, then there will inevitably come a time when a 'second wind' is needed. Athletics is a great example, as you watch the long-distance runners go lap, after lap, after lap, in a gruelling race, which gets faster and faster, the nearer to the finishing line the runners get. I am sure that these long distance runners, despite feelings of exhaustion, find that 'second wind' that takes them to and over the finishing line.

When sparring with Gabriel, a forbidding, heavyweight sized fellow, with years of martial arts experience from all over the world, the 'second wind' is much needed. Just imagine; I am trying to focus on executing my punches and kicks, elbows and knees, with accuracy and precision. At the same time, I am focusing on Gabriel's next move. I swiftly move about, after all, as a ten stone lightweight (considerably lighter than Gabriel) I have the speed, whilst he most definitely has the power. He comes towards me and I stick my leg out, aiming for his stomach to try and slow him down, then I move around. It works – this time! But he comes at me again and this time my leg, despite driving as much energy and force through it as possible, doesn't fully stop Gabriel in his tracks and he is right there in front of me, holding me. I hold on to him and take a few very deep breathes in and out and I summon the 'second wind', twist him off me and continue to focus on the task at hand.

Rather than continually referring to this newly released and realised energy as the 'second wind', I am going to call it, 're-forming the lines of battle'. With the depiction of the sparring session with Gabriel in mind, having taken those deep breathes for ten seconds, the fighter re-forms his lines of battle, including his lines of defence.

There is no greater foe than cancer and it will continue to do battle with each and every person it attacks. It will keep coming forward and it will keep punching and kicking. But it is no one's friend, there in front of you to guide you, to train you, to give you confidence and make you a better person. The cancer will not do that.

The fight comes from within every person and one has to focus on the fight. Not the knees and elbows, punches and kicks, but the chemotherapy and radiotherapy, the operations, the medicines, the travelling to and from the hospital, the loneliness, the feelings of despair. All of these need combating in one way or another and there will inevitably be times, when the lines of battle will certainly need to be re-formed.

I can clearly remember the immense pain and feelings of sickness brought on by the chemotherapy and radiotherapy, which I was given simultaneously for a period of seven weeks (not to mention a second batch of radiotherapy after the cancer in my neck was removed). The first few sessions with this duo of debilitating, but much needed drugs, were harsh and the feelings of despair were great. Yet, I knew I had weeks of treatment still ahead of me and I braced myself for what was to come, by setting my mind to re-forming the lines of battle. I rallied every day, taking stock of what I had been through and telling myself that the fight was on and I needed to be ready for the next onslaught the following day, the day after that and so on…and on…and on.

The battle with feelings invoked by this hideous foe, means that one's mind must be set to a future, in which there is no more cancer and therefore, no more treatments and feelings of gloom. When one has to call on the help, of the positivity of life and the comfort from friends and family, professionals and other people who care, it is then, that the battle lines are re-formed over and over again, to the extent that the enemy becomes weaker and weaker, pathetic and insubstantial. This mind set will help one to find their 'second wind' and then use it with full force, to pulverise and pound the cancer into oblivion.

In another one of my favourite films, *Lord of the Rings - The Return of the King* (based on J.R.R Tolkien's book), Theoden, King of Rohan, assembles a huge army to do battle with the Orcs who have stormed Gondor. The Orcs are a huge army of nasty, creature-like soldiers whose lack of fighting skills, make their large numbers one of their only advantages. As the Rohirrim (the horse riders of Rohan) and their fellow soldiers, who have joined them in their battle to free Middle-Earth of this putrid and vile enemy, gather, the battle cries which the King shouts out, just before they attack the Orcs, are indeed memorable. Just listening to these cries, invokes feelings of inspiration and encouragement. But it is the rallying cries of 'Re-form the line, re-form the line', following their initial attack, which sees every soldier re-grouping and readying themselves to attack once more, that are the most meaningful to me. Whether having read the book or seen the film, the end result, is victory for all who hold true to goodness and light.

It is surprising, that I only met Gabriel some 15 years after the radio and chemotherapy, the operations and struggles, but I innately applied the method of the 'second wind' to my situation at that time. Years later, Gabriel showed me how crucial re-forming the line is, in one's fight with cancer. We all, without exception, have an ability to 're-form the line' and this ability must be deployed throughout our lives, not least in the fight with cancer.

Equipped for Working in a School (speaking to teachers, parents, colleagues from other schools, governors and children)

Ever since I was 15-years-old, when I went to see the careers advisor at my secondary school, I knew that I wanted to be a teacher, a guide and role model to primary school children. Until that moment, I hadn't really thought too hard about what I wanted to focus on when I left school, including which subject I would study at university. It was the careers advisor at the school I attended, who pointed me in the direction of teaching as a profession. I can't say that I had ever really contemplated teaching as a career, but the suggestion really appealed to me and I began to research education as a vocation. (A school was the ideal place to seek advice and gather information!) I sat my A Levels, took a gap year and then went to university to study primary school teaching. I started my career as a class teacher in a two-form entry primary school and I was really keen to move up the ranks as quickly as I could, without, of course, rushing the vital steps only experience can give, to senior leadership positions.

I moved on from being a class teacher in one school, to being a class teacher with responsibilities, as deputy of a department within another, larger, three-form entry primary school. This was indeed, a different sort of experience and the work was rigorous and demanding, although no more so, than a class teacher who takes home literally, piles of marking every evening and most school holidays. Yet being a senior leader, who is forever being held to account, increased my stress levels and this certainly added to the enormity of the task of helping to lead a department.

My career moved on, as I became the director of a department at school and assistant head teacher, with the responsibility for a diverse range of tasks and duties, all of which required a degree of verbal interaction. From speaking to a parent on the phone, to standing in the school hall and talking to 700 children, about a variety of important topics, for example, the heroes of the First World War, on Armistice Day every year (this is just an example of one assembly of many, in the course of an academic year).

To be honest, talking to someone face-to-face, as opposed to emailing, texting, or even phoning them, is my preferred mode of communication. I feel that I can get the best results for both parties, when I am having a face-to-face dialogue. Whether it is with a parent, a member of staff, a senior colleague or a governor, I feel more at ease with an 'in the flesh' conversation. Nonetheless, it is somewhat ironic, that this should be my preferred mode of communication, when I can now get extremely conscious of my facial disabilities.

There are governors' meetings and the meetings with colleagues from other education establishments, when it is usual to have coffee and cake. Perhaps even a sandwich lunch, at which all those present will have a hearty conversation, whilst biting into an egg-filled wrap or a cream cake, topped with cherries or a strawberry for decoration. However, my mouth opening, being very limited, means that I simply cannot contemplate eating, whilst talking. For me, a cream cake needs to be eaten with care and precision, if it is to enter my mouth without the contents finding their way on to my upper lip or indeed other parts of my face! (As I have no nerves on my upper lip and right cheek and therefore no sensation or feeling, I wouldn't feel the cream, on the one place the cream is most likely to find its way to!)

So I reach for the flat biscuit, the size of which will easily be 'popped' into my mouth, without causing me any embarrassment. Or the small, seedless olive or slice of pickled cucumber, which can be eaten ever so simply. Still, there is the conversation I am about to have; this will now be far simpler for me and cause me no worry or concern about being impolite whilst eating.

As I was growing up, I remember my parents being excellent role models in how to eat and speak with impeccable manners and I have tried, all my life, particularly when in the presence of others, to follow in their 'well-mannered' footsteps. So, trying to eat, while at the same time conversing with a colleague, is not a good combination for me.

To eat in front of people I don't know, is most difficult, but eating and then teaching, presents its own challenges, with a complex mouth such as mine. When eating anything solid, I have to regularly rinse my mouth out. But not as one would simply go to the bathroom, take a swig of water or mouthwash, spit it out, clean the sink down and then three or four minutes later the mouth is clean. I have to take my prosthesis out of my mouth, clean it, put it back, rinse my mouth out (with water pouring through my nose!) and then when all that is done, hope and pray that no left-over water trickles or drips down my nose, whilst I am explaining to the children, the learning objectives of the next lesson.

Nevertheless, teaching on an empty stomach is not the wisest of options either and I needed to find a solution to my challenging situation. After all, not eating properly has all sorts of knock-on effects. To employ the 'fighting spirit' you need energy; you can't fight on an empty stomach.

I therefore established a daily eating routine which, whilst not perfect, would see me satiated through the day, until I arrived home from a day's work and could eat something wholesome at my own leisure. Every morning, I was to eat a large bowl of wholesome cereal, whilst at lunchtime I would have vegetable soup and a roll, with a couple of yoghurts, together with vegetable or fruit juices. Whilst not perfect, it at least gave me enough energy to preserve my drive at work, until I arrived home.

This deficiency in my abilities to eat and drink were further emphasised, when speaking to a couple of Year 6 pupils, just after lunch one day. I had gone into the school's dining room to get my vegetable soup and roll and after exchanging pleasantries with the catering staff and speaking to a handful of children about a variety of things, I went back in to my office to eat. I must have felt quite brave as there was a knock on my door and one of the school receptionists poked her head around the door. 'There are a couple of Year 6 pupils outside, who would like to speak to you about the end of year graduation; can I send them in to you?' I immediately (and somewhat bravely) replied in the affirmative and the two children strolled happily into my office and sat down to speak to me.

Now, at this point I had just taken a few bites of my roll and had swallowed the contents and armed with a tissue, was busily (but not frantically or awkwardly) wiping my face, in case of any stray crumbs, or anything bigger! The two children began to ask their question, after which, I proceeded to give them an answer. As I did so, a lone piece of dough-like substance found its way to the front of my mouth and up on to the top of my upper lip. 'I remember swallowing the full contents which was inside my mouth and I have just wiped my mouth, so how could this have happened?' I thought to myself, as I rather sheepishly turned my 'swivel' chair around and reached for another tissue. As I wiped this lone offender from my lip, I breathed an inner sigh of relief. I'm pretty sure that the two children did not notice anything, because they happily left my office, clearly satisfied with the answer I had given them.

When all is said and done, I am amazed by children's innocence and their ability to look at a person for who and what they really are, rather than judging (as adults too often do) a 'book by its cover', or a person by the way they appear outwardly. Not one child has ever said to me anything at all about my face, even though one can easily recognise a facial defect on my right-hand side, compared to the number of adults who, whilst not verbalising it, certainly look askance.

Indeed, during my many visits to the hospital for dental check-ups and treatments, for check-ups with the surgeons and for yearly scans, I have often seen fellow patients who have obvious defects in their face and who, when chatting to them in the waiting room, are such lovely, approachable people. I recall contacting a charity which supported people who had experienced facial disfigurements as a result of facial cancers. The lady I spoke to and subsequently met, was the nicest of people you could ever meet.

She was softly spoken and her words of care were comforting, as she shared her experiences with me. How often do we look at people in the street, in the supermarket, in the bank and in the doctor's surgery and cast immediate aspersions on them? Without having ever spoken to them, just because of the way they look. We all too often, make shallow decisions and snap judgments about people and once again, it had taught me that 'appearances can be deceiving'. I am truly grateful that I chose the teaching profession, working with young people who seem to innately know not to just look at the surface, but at what is beyond.

'If you focus on the finger, you will miss all that heavenly glory'

When a fighter steps into the ring, for a fight he has been preparing for over a long period of time, he usually enters the ring to a cacophony of noise, loud music and a cheering crowd. Whilst the music is often chosen by the entering fighter, usually as a means of encouragement, the rest of the noise is merely background noise. I recall a similar experience when going for my black belt and particularly, the two verses one spar, for which I had prepared diligently.

Over the course of the past six months leading up to my black belt grading, I had trained for my forthcoming encounter with two brown belts, assiduously. At the end of my two hour, weekly lessons with Steven, we would stay on past the official end of the lesson, together with a couple of friends, to train for the two against one encounter. I remember at the time, being ever so grateful to the caretaker of the hall we used, as she often left her house and came downstairs to lock up, at close to midnight. Steven explained to me a clever manoeuvre, in which I would outsmart the two opponents, whereby they would be obliged to attack me one at a time, as opposed to two attackers at once. As one opponent tried to move around, so would I and thus maintain the 'one behind the other' effect. This ensured I was only having to, effectively, fight one person at a time.

Funnily enough, when I had seen the video of Steven's two against one spar (not forgetting that he was a heavyweight, with a lot of power), he had made it his aim to dispense with one of the two fighters, thus enabling him to focus on just one. As the video shows, Steven did just that; he knocked one of the opponents down and whilst this bewildered and bemused opponent staggered back to his feet, he was visibly shaken for the remainder of the two minute fight.

Being a lightweight, I had more speed than power and I could move quickly, whilst keeping my opponents at bay. I knew that the strategy I had to adopt was to keep them both in a line and not allow them to both be in front of me at the same time. (Steven had advised me to make a quick judgement as to who was the slightly weaker of the two and keep him in front at all times.) I went into the spar with this mantra stamped on to my mind; 'Keep one in front of the other, keep one in front of the other,' over and over again. But with the best intentions, the fatigue, weariness and fight for survival, sometimes allows one's mind to stray off course.

I therefore, kept focused on Steven's voice throughout my 'twin' encounter, as he kept repeating, 'Keep them in a line, keep them in a line,' over and over again. I can assure you, that there were a large number of people, during those two minutes, all shouting one thing or another. But the one voice I focused on was Steven's, repeatedly encouraging me not to enable my opponents to simultaneously both come face-to-face with me.

I first watched another of my favourite martial arts movies, *Enter the Dragon*, when I was about 13-years-old and I enjoyed it so much, that I never get bored of the fight scenes and Bruce Lee's famous philosophical lines. Whilst not part of the main plot in the story, there was one line which really made an impression on me, ever since I first watched the film. I would repeat this line again and again, as I was accustomed to doing, having watched a film which I enjoyed. Whilst pointing upwards with his index finger, Bruce Lee tells his young student to look up at the night sky, the moon and the stars. The student proceeds to look at Bruce Lee's finger, to which Lee responds by gently chastising his young pupil with a tap on the head and says, '…if you focus on the finger, you will miss all that heavenly glory.'

The fight with cancer is usually long and hard, with the war only won when many a battle has taken place. When the exactitudes of radiotherapy are done, when the rigour of chemotherapy has reached its crescendo, when the enormity of the painful operations have been overcome and when you have a grip on the ever increasing roller-coaster of emotions, then you can hesitate and take stock. The war is not over, but the battle has been won. The war will never be over and it is that fact that must remain your focus. Ask anyone who has fought and overcome this horrible disease, when they first hear the doctor or surgeon declare, 'You are in remission,' or 'It has been successfully removed,' it goes some way to giving you a sense of relief and a modicum of reprieve. But don't lose sight of the real picture. Don't stray from the actual truth that – yes, you have just overcome the most adverse of foes and you have just won battles, so bravely and valiantly fought. But don't lose your focus on the on-going job to be done. There may be other tumours lurking while you are unaware. To misplace this sense of reality, to stray from the awareness that one has just overcome the most adverse of foes, is to lose focus on the job at hand.

Look beyond the finger pointing to the sky and focus on the sky itself. Look at the bigger picture, the battles you have valiantly fought and so bravely won. But, don't lose sight of the bigger picture and instead keep focusing on the two opponents who would rather you didn't keep them at bay, who would rather you didn't keep them one behind the other. Rejoice in the victory and shout it from the rooftops. Be ecstatic, but retain that focus on the continuing war, on keeping the cancer away by whichever means that are within your power.

I'll always remember a speech my mother gave at a dinner we held following my 'all clear', giving us the chance to thank God for helping us through these challenging times and the opportunity to thank the numerous people, whose kindness and care had been so instrumental in aiding my recovery. As part of this speech, my mother said, '...a spot will never just be a spot again and a pimple will never just be a pimple...' and all these years later, these words are embedded on my mind. For those who have valiantly fought and overcome cancer, a lot is going on around you and the demands of your profession are great. A return to a 'normal' life means the hustle and bustle of daily demands, deadlines, protocol and short and long term targets. But stay focused on your key objective; keep the cancer away.

Returning to the Spirit of the Fight

To be honest, I am not the biggest football fan in the world, although I do enjoy watching the weekly highlights and following various teams, as they compete and eventually race for the title each season, between August of one year and May the following year. One of my highpoints in the football season is when the football analysts choose the 'Goal of the Season', where a series of the best goals are chosen by expert pundits and aired, much to the delight of many a football fanatic. The latest 'Goal of the Season' which I watched at the end of the last football season , produced some remarkable and exceptional goals, as well as some even more noteworthy celebrations, by the goal-scorers themselves.

One significant celebration portrayed by a majority of the goal-scorers was a finger gesture skyward, pointing one or both forefingers towards heaven and mumbling something under their breath, as they turned and ran ecstatically away from their opponents' goal mouth. Even before sprinting at full speed to their team mates and celebrating their personal feat with a fist in the air and wild celebrations (depending, of course, on the nature of the match), they first showed a kind of 'spiritual' response.

I am not a professional footballer and I don't even play it in the park anymore (I did in my teenage years!), but one thing that is clear, is the pressure that these players are under, to win matches. After all, an awful lot of money is riding on their successes. Therefore, I can only imagine that it is the utter relief and the amazing euphoria, at scoring a goal that could possibly win an award (or more than one award) for the team, which invokes such a 'spiritual' response, followed by, of course, a very overjoyed and jubilant celebration with comrades.

As a school teacher and as part of the statutory 'communal daily worship', I often lead the morning assembly and encourage the children in their spiritual conversations. In the very materialistic world we live in nowadays, children, understandably, very often find it difficult to recognise the need to perform this daily act of prayer and are often turned off the idea, that praying to a superpower will bear any fruit, whatsoever. So, I showed one group of children a series of goals being scored and they witnessed with their own eyes how the initial celebrations of one footballer after another, was a gaze heavenward, followed by a short and silent prayer. If you had been given the opportunity of witnessing those children's responses to my rather unconventional explanation, you would have seen the enlightenment on their faces, as if they were, at last, able to associate the meaning of what prayer is and what it potentially can do for a person.

Like the goal-scoring footballer, I will forever thank God, the name I give to my all-powerful being, along with millions of others across the globe. Not for the comparative triviality of enabling me to score a goal (although to a professional footballer, scoring a goal is far from trivial), but for the blessing of courage, to keep fighting a disease which is relentless in its malicious desire to destroy.

My belief, that each kind of fight has a spiritual side to it, was made even firmer, when I happened to watch an interview with a fighter, who has become one of my most inspirational boxers: Evander Holyfield.

Evander Holyfield was such an inspiration to me, that when my parents kindly paid for me to have some sessions with a sports psychologist (a couple of months before my black belt grading), I would visualise the images of Holyfield's fighting technique as an inner source of encouragement. Even on the day of my black belt grading, Holyfield's style was imprinted on my mind.

Having already become champion of the world in the cruiserweight division, Holyfield went on to become heavyweight champion of the world. He was the only boxer to win the world heavyweight titles four times (on Holyfield's official website, it claims he was five times Heavyweight world champion) and on 13th November 1992, Holyfield fought his friend and sparring partner, Riddick Bowe, during a defence of his world titles. Holyfield subsequently lost that fight, but a year later he was back in the ring with Bowe and on 6th November 1993, Holyfield reclaimed the title, heavyweight champion of the world.

Having lost the first bout with Riddick Bowe, Holyfield explains in an interview, how he introduced a very 'real' element of spirituality in to his life.

He explains that he would often hear the term 'prayer' used out of habit. Children are told to pray for something, adults are told to pray for this or pray for that; but it is only when one truly yearns for something, when one is so desperate (as Holyfield was, to reclaim the title) and wants something so much, so badly, that Holyfield terms this type of prayer as 'real' and not uttered out of habit.

I can truly identify with this notion of prayer and apply it to my own journey through life's ups and downs. There are clearly occasions which I would prefer not to experience, like the days in school when a pupil is sent to me for misbehaving, or a member of staff is off sick and a supply teacher needs to be found, to cover their lessons for the day. When I am standing in a shop, waiting in a queue behind a customer whose credit card is not being validated by the card machine and therefore delaying the whole aisle. Yes, I raise my eyes heavenward and ask for help, but I am not desperate and my prayer reflects these unperturbed feelings.

But when my very life is at stake and my own personal heavyweight title bout is on the line, my prayers are uttered with a fervour which is incomparable to those prayers expressed as a result of those irritating and comparatively insignificant episodes. It is during these 'real' episodes in my life, when it is literally my existence which is on the line, that the fervour and desperation makes the prayer a powerful energy in linking the physical and the spiritual, thus creating a dynamic drive of optimism and positivity.

Timing is Everything

As I was progressing through the different coloured belts, towards the much coveted black belt (a feat I had always longed to accomplish, ever since the moment I first stepped into the martial arts class), one progressively difficult test which was part of the overall examination, was the sparring. As part of the 'grading' (the term used for the examination for each progressive belt), I would have to 'spar' an opponent. Admittedly, the only spar which was full contact was at the black belt grading, when 16oz boxing gloves and a head guard were worn. The sparring for the other belts would consist of mainly kicks and punches to the body. In fact, the examiners made it clear that they wanted to see evidence that a person could attack, but also successfully defend themselves without being backed into a corner, resulting in the spar having to be paused and then restarted from the centre of the room. As my opponent and I came face-to-face with each other, the referee (usually an instructor) gave the command to 'bow' and then 'free-spar'. This encounter would always last for two minutes; not a second more or a second less.

Similarly, when a boxer hears the call for the 'seconds out' and he comes back into the centre of the ring for another gruelling three minute round, he knows that it's going to be exactly three minutes. He has trained long and hard to overcome that feeling of utter exhaustion. He has trained for those three minutes of fighting and that one minute of rest. He knows at which point to apply the extra pressure, because the round is nearing its end, or when to minimise his exertion, because there is still a considerable part of the round remaining. The fighter also knows at which point it's best to attack or counter-attack and he sees his opportunity and times it to perfection, or else suffers the possible devastating consequences.

As well as the feeling of immense fatigue from the continuous moving and execution of punches, kicks and knees, there is the application of a huge amount of concentration on the opponent's next move. When I am fighting Gabriel, I look into his eyes and I carefully scan his posture and movement and attempt to anticipate his next move. I see his hand leave its defensive position next to his face, exposing a gap and I punch. Then I see him come forward towards me with a kick and I step out of the way, wait for his leg to land on the ground and just at that very moment, I attack. Not a second before or a second later, or else, once again, suffer the potential consequences.

When engaging this malignant enemy, timing is so important in the overall fight. Primarily, it is the first diagnosis which is often so crucial and can give a person an immediate advantage. Don't waste time; if you think you have felt something untoward, get it looked at as soon as possible, because the earlier it is caught, the less difficult the fight and the better the outcome. Then there are the timings of the different treatments (as in my case, when the doctors and surgeons agreed that the chemo and radiotherapies should come first and then the tumour's removal); the precision of the radiotherapy, with its pinpoint accuracy; the exact dosage of the chemotherapy drugs, according to a person's height and weight, as they carefully pass through the drip on the way to confront the enemy; the strict schedule in taking the anti-sickness pills and the meticulous timing for taking the ever so important painkillers, allowing for those desperately needed moments of reprieve.

Moreover, in preparation for the surgery to remove the tumour, the ever so skilful surgeons had to determine their every move. I can only imagine the precision needed when they operated on my face and I certainly don't take any part of that surgery for granted. To have to manoeuvre around such delicate areas, such as the eyes, nose, mouth, teeth and ears, must be no easy matter to say the least and certainly takes years of training. To have to quickly and carefully look through a microscope at each piece of tumour being removed, until the magnified pieces of cut away tissue and flesh no longer reveal any tumorous growth. Yes, the procedure must have been a very bloody and gruesome scene to behold, but the precision of the surgeon's knife and alert eye overshadow this and for that, I will be forever thankful.

For the fighter, timing is everything in their quest for success and that includes the fighter who is standing 'toe-to-toe' with an intangible opponent, such as cancer. But there is one big difference. When the fighters step into the ring or respectfully bow to one another, the clock will start and the seconds counted down. There will be a winner and there will be a loser, but both will (eventually, if the victory hasn't been achieved through a knock-out!) be standing either side of the referee. The hideous aim of cancer is to cause devastation, knocking the patient off their feet and the timing of every move must be done with the height of precision and accuracy.

How Can I Cope Without You?

From the moment I was diagnosed with cancer and a treatment plan quickly drawn up and organised for me, not only did the hospital become like my second home, but it also became a tremendous source of reassurance.

For seven weeks, I went to the hospital every day, except for weekends (apart from when I 'checked-in' to the ward on a Sunday evening, for surgery the next morning) and for ten months I was a regular visitor. I would go to see the oncologists, the surgeons, the dieticians, the specialist dentists, the radiographers and the ear, nose and throat specialists and every single one of these professionals, including the nurses, medical assistants, porters and other carers, made me feel secure and comforted. If I experienced an ache or pain, I could consult someone at the hospital. If I needed reassurance about a potential side-effect to any of the treatments or medicines, I could get it there and then, without having to phone a helpline, or call an appointment team to organise a much needed appointment with a very busy medical professional.

One might have thought that the trips to and from the hospital to have radiotherapy and the days and nights I spent on hospital wards were irritating and frustrating. I suppose they were to an extent, in light of the pain, feelings of loneliness and overall fear of the unknown. But, in a funny sort of way and with high insight, I valued those times in the hospital and when I was at home, would often long for the immediate care and support of the medical professionals.

Having spoken to other recovering cancer patients, about the attention they received from the caring medical specialists, they have all told me about these feelings of emptiness and loneliness; that a part of their daily routine is missing and how they ultimately worry for the future, without the much valued day to day support.

But, like many other episodes in our lives, which come and go, it is those valued and treasured moments which must be cherished and embraced. By taking these moments into the future with us, we carve a pathway of clarity, where the experiences of the past help us to build our future. The attention and professionalism of the medical teams who cared for us, are still available to offer advice and continued support. Now we must take the opportunity to continue living our lives, not stifled by the rigours of treatments, but with the assurance that, waiting in the wings, those compassionate health professionals will always be there for us. As long as we remember where we have come from, we can approach the future with optimism.

As soon as I came out into the light, having travelled through the dark tunnel of cancer, I knew what I needed to do for the future - to deploy the 'fighting spirit'. I would do everything in my power to keep the cancer far from me. I would eat healthily, do regular exercise, try ever so hard to get my work/life balance right and put life's experiences into perspective, especially the somewhat negative experiences. I would use the 'fighting spirit' to carve a path through life's ups and downs and I would cherish the thought of knowing that my inner belief system has the ability to tap in to a higher power, as a source of comfort and reassurance.

There is a parable told (in a world long before cars, when the only mode of transport was by horse or foot), of a villager who had never left the comforts of his hometown, but now desired to leave his town and head to a faraway city. He carefully packed his bags, making sure to pack every provision for the long journey into the unknown. The night before he was to set off on his unfamiliar sojourn, he went to the local Tavern for a farewell drink with all his friends. His supportive comrades all wished him much luck on his journey, whilst reminding him about the provisions he would need.

'Have you remembered to pack a map?' came one quiet suggestion from the corner of the pub. The traveller, rather haughtily and over-confidently responded, that a map was not necessary. He would simply follow the signposts along the way, until he reached his destination.

The next morning, the traveller set off on his adventure and just as he had said, he followed each signpost which pointed him in the direction of his journey's end. All was going well until he came to a crossroads, but instead of the signpost standing upright, it lay flat on the ground, having been knocked over. The traveller looked at it and scratched his head, but this bold and brave fellow was no fool. On the contrary. He knew the name of the town he had come from and therefore, picked up the signpost and stuck it back into the ground, with the name of his hometown pointing in the right direction. At once, all three other directions fell perfectly into place. One must be fully aware from where they have come, so as to successfully navigate their continued journey, into the future.

If a person can use the 'fighting spirit' in their determination to overcome cancer, then every subsequent obstacle that comes their way can be fended off. They must remember from where they have come, the moment of diagnosis and being told 'It is cancer,' the weeks of treatment, the feelings of fatigue and sickness, the operations and the roller coaster of emotions. Now it is time to forge a path through what life has on offer, but always use the past experiences to move on, into the future.

In Perfect Synchronisation

Ever since the maxillectomy (the operation to remove the cancer from my right maxillary sinus and part of my nose, cheekbone, half the hard palate and teeth), I was always fully aware about how restricted my mouth opening was and the complications it would and does cause me. Nevertheless, the associated problems were further highlighted on one of my subsequent visits to the hospital, to see the specialist dentist.

One of my upper molar teeth on the left-hand side of my mouth, was causing me a lot of discomfort and considering I found it virtually impossible to eat on the right side of my mouth, I needed to have an urgent consultation with the specialist dentist at the hospital. He proceeded to look in my mouth and saw that indeed, there was a hole in one of the previously filled upper molars, but towards the very back of my mouth. I can only describe to you, as best I can, how brilliant this dentist is, at manoeuvring the variety of dental hand-pieces (to which a drill is attached) around my mouth, into spaces that are so small, even a hand-piece used for a child wouldn't fit. He sees people like me all the time, but that still doesn't detract from the dexterity which he has developed during his years of experience.

I could almost guess what he was about to tell me and I was proved correct, when he explained, that due to the position of the hole in the tooth, as well as the tooth already being heavily filled (too many sweets as a teenager!), the best option was to have it removed altogether. He continued to explain that an extra tooth would be added to my mouth-piece, which would fit into place perfectly, following the extraction. He told me that the tooth would be best taken out under general anaesthetic, as this would enable the surgeons to get my mouth open much wider.

I thanked the dentist and headed for the Tube station, contemplating the forthcoming operation to extract the tooth. It was at that moment that it suddenly dawned on me; how will the obturator fit in my mouth straight after the procedure to remove the decayed tooth? How long would I be without a mouth-piece, unable to eat, drink and unable to speak?

I arrived home and immediately phoned the hospital and spoke to the dentist, who most kindly reassured me that the ever so important mouth-piece would be altered whilst I was in the operating theatre having the tooth out.

The doctors and surgeons at the hospital are superb, the nurses are so caring, the dentist is amazing and now it was the turn of my wife, to be an added brilliance in the overall process of having this troublesome tooth taken out. However, the synchronisation had to be spot-on, so that I could wake up from the GA, gather my thoughts and then be able to speak, eat and drink properly.

The 'Tooth Extraction Day' came and my wife and I took the Tube up to the hospital. When we arrived, we made our way to the Maxillofacial ward and were shown to my room. It's always nice having your own room on a hospital ward, but I have never really minded being on a ward with other people, as it's more vibrant. There's lots more going on, people coming and going and there's less chance of getting lonely and all the subsequent feelings loneliness can conjure up.

My wife and I settled down; I got changed into a hospital gown which, even to this day, I could never quite work out how to put on and my wife sat down and took her book out to read. She very lovingly and reassuringly kept asking me if I was feeling alright and I responded with a nervous 'Yes, I'm OK,' giving me a feeling of comfort and support at each time of asking.

However, the one burning thought on my mind was the mouth-piece and I carefully dipped my hand into my rucksack, to feel for the hard, protective case in which I always kept it, on the rare occasion it wasn't in my mouth. I took it out of my bag, took the mouth-piece out of my mouth, placing it prudently into the shielding case and reached over and handed it to my wife. From the way in which I handed it to her, one might have thought there was a diamond inside which was worth a small fortune. To me, the mouth-piece was invaluable and the care with which I always handled it and certainly held it at that moment, reflected the priceless nature of this life-changing and most effective device. She opened the case, took the obturator out and handed it back to me. 'You're going to need this until you are taken down to the operating theatre,' my wife, quite rightly, responded and I duly put it back into my mouth.

It was a good job that I was able to speak once more, as I reminded my wife of the plan to get the extra bits added to the palatal obturator in good time for when I awoke. The hospital had informed the nearby laboratory that someone would be coming on such and such a day, with an existing mouth-piece, so that some minor alterations and additions could be made, in line with an extraction which would be carried out at the same time. As soon as I was down in the operating theatre, my wife would make her way (by taxi, to avoid the undoubted wait for a bus) to the laboratory and hand them the 'diamond'. She would then wait until they had completed their modifications and catch a taxi back to the hospital and my bedside.

Of course, only my wife can tell you the whole story of the visit to the lab, but there she was when I came around after the general anaesthetic, sitting by my bed, smiling. After what seemed like a few minutes, I asked my wife for the obturator and she carefully handed it to me, with a great big smile on her face. I cautiously placed it in my mouth, my hands shaking slightly, praying under my breath that it would fit as planned and I bit down on it. The plan to remove my molar tooth, whilst getting the palatal obturator updated, had been done with perfect synchronisation.

I'm a Winner Inside and a Winner Outside

Another one of my boxing heroes and one who truly inspires me, is Michael Watson MBE. Born in Hackney in 1965, Watson became the British Commonwealth middleweight champion in 1989, beating Nigel Benn to win the title. One fight led to another and eventually Watson was given a shot at the middleweight world title against champion Chris Eubank. His first encounter with Eubank went the course of the twelve rounds, with Watson very narrowly losing on the judges' score cards, 116-113, 115-113 and 114-114.

This was such a close score, that many boxing experts and commentators demanded a rematch. So, Eubank and Watson were to have a second go, three months later on 21st September 1991 and this time at White Hart Lane, the home of Tottenham Hotspur Football Club. Both boxers climbed back into the ring and after eleven rounds, Watson knocked Eubank down. But he got back up within the ten second count and a couple of minutes later, caught Watson with a huge punch to the head. Watson was knocked out and fell backwards, hitting his head against the ropes surrounding the ring. At the end of the bout Watson collapsed, was rushed to hospital and spent the next 40 days in a coma and the extent of his injuries meant that he had to undergo no fewer than six brain operations to remove a blood clot.

Watson's neurosurgeon, Mr Peter Hamlyn, said about him, 'I think back to those first days and the milestone moments. The first eight months were so depressing. He,' referring to Watson, 'couldn't hear, couldn't speak, couldn't walk. Slowly, he clawed it all back. So extraordinary.'

Michael Watson is someone I look up to, as too, do many others. Not necessarily for his boxing skills, although he had these aplenty, but because he is someone who has an immense ability to fight against adversity. His fight to regain all his faculties, his power of speech, his hearing and walking, was huge and many would have written him off. In fact, before his fateful second bout with Chris Eubank, Michael Watson said, 'I'm a winner inside and a winner outside.' Whilst he would certainly never have chosen to demonstrate his inner fighting skills in such an adverse way, Watson most certainly had the opportunity to demonstrate his winning qualities, both inside and out and he continues to do so, to be an inspiration to all those 'fighters' out there.

I am just one of millions of people who have stared cancer in the face and overcome this retched illness and all that it leaves behind. I have been in the thick of it, when the fight is just starting and I have been in the midst of the fight and am now living with the after-effects. So take heed; with the right 'corner-men' (God to pray to, a sympathetic wife and other close members of the family who listen, doctors who offer advice and medication, surgeons who perform their amazing handiwork, nurses who show their enormous amount of care and medical skills, dieticians, physiotherapists, technicians, someone who is a good listener), with the right medication and with the correct use of the mind, I will always try my utmost to 'claw' my way back in to any fight which comes my way, especially the fight for life.

An Encouraging Thought

If you were to go to my parents' home, into the kitchen and then walk toward the fridge, you would witness an unusual sight. Most people (myself included) may have the odd magnet stuck here and there or perhaps some 'frenzied-fridge-magnet person' may have a whole plethora of magnetic memorabilia from every holiday they had ever been on. But if you would simply stand next to one of the sides of this tall, grey metallic fridge, you would read quotes. Not just one or two quotes, but many quotes from books and films which are, in one way or another, very significant to any reader.

This quote-laden side of the refrigerator is regularly updated, as my mother reads or hears a poignant line or sentence from a book or film. She types it out, laminates it and sticks it to the side of her fridge for all to read. Then, whenever someone asks for her advice, be it family or friend, she will end the conversation by asking them to read such and such a particular quote which is on the fridge. Once the family member or friend has had a short, but meaningful chat with my parents and then goes over to the fridge to read the quote, the resulting feeling is often one of insight and deep reflection. I know this to be true, because of the many conversations I have had with my parents, followed by, 'Now, just go to the fridge and have a good look at that quote on the left, about half way down...'

I would like to share one of these quotes with you, in fact my favourite quote and then explain why it is one of my much-loved quotations. Many people are familiar with J.R.R. Tolkien's *Lord of the Rings* (which I have already mentioned in an earlier chapter) and the recent movies which were based on his books. In the first book/movie, *The Fellowship of the Ring*, a group of daring and brave individuals are chosen to help Frodo Baggins destroy the 'One Ring' of evil and this group of comrades set out on their quest to rid the world of all wickedness. Whilst his companions will do whatever they can to protect him from harm, it is only Frodo himself, who has been charged with the responsibility of taking the ring to a specific fiery chasm in a place called Mordor, where he must throw it in to the molten lava below, to destroy it.

As he starts out on his perilous journey, he stops to reflect on his suitability for such an onerous task. He contemplates why he, of all people, had to be chosen to destroy the ring of evil. Frodo says to his friend and mentor, the wise wizard, Gandalf the Grey, 'I wish the ring had never come to me. I wish none of this had happened.' To which Gandalf replies, 'So do all who live to see such times. But that is not for them to decide. All we have to decide, is what to do with the time that is given to us. There are other forces at work in this world, Frodo, besides the will of evil. Bilbo was meant to find the ring. In which case, you were also meant to have it and that, is an encouraging thought.'

As people on this earth embark on their life's journey, many of them believe (and it's not just a religious belief) that everything happens for a reason and that everyone has a fate. For some people, it is a higher power that controls this fate, but everyone, inevitably has a destiny.

During both times I was diagnosed with cancer, one of the many thoughts rushing through my head was, 'Why me? Why did this have to happen to me?' As I mentioned in an earlier chapter, you start to question why you were chosen to get this most dreaded of illnesses. I was just twenty six-years of age and I had lived a pretty healthy life, so why was I the lucky, chosen one!

But then this quote from the side of the tall grey fridge speaks to me, '...you were meant to have it...' and it's difficult to argue with that. If, as I believe, everyone has a fate or a destiny, then thinking that there is a reason (unbeknown to me at the time) I was meant to get cancer, then that is a somewhat soothing thought. It is important for me to reiterate, that it took some time before I was fortified by the notion that my illness was 'meant to be' and that it was my destiny. For some, it may never become clear as to why they were struck with such a malevolent illness, but for the majority, that clarity will eventually prevail.

A small twist in my destiny (some would say that it was a 'big' twist!), came shortly after I divorced my first wife, about five years after the treatments and operations to rid me of the cancer. I will not labour the point, other than to say, we walked away from each other amicably, with the agreement that we would do the best for our four children and we continue to do so, until this very day. Some months later, I was told by a close friend, rather excitedly, that there was a lovely lady she thought I should meet and that we were really suited for each other. She duly wrote her mobile phone number on a piece of paper which I folded and carefully placed in my coat pocket.

I picked up the telephone receiver with a small amount of trepidation, but also curiosity, to hear this lady's voice and subsequently meet her. The dialling tones sounded and after about four or five rings, she answered her phone. She seemed so delighted to hear my voice and the elation in her voice came across to me as tones of genuine relief and happiness. Of course, I was a little confused, but her next few sentences explained it all.

My new wife-to-be described how, a short while ago, when she was training to be a dental nurse in a local medical institution, together with a few dozen other trainee nurses, the tutors gave them an opportunity to observe for a few weeks in a Maxillofacial department of a local hospital. My wife-to-be, was one of the handful of students who volunteered to observe at the Maxillofacial Unit and it was while she was there, that she saw me. She had remembered my name and most of all, how the surgeons showed me how to place the obturator in and out of my mouth and how I struggled with my limited mouth opening. She remembered seeing the look of worry on my face, yet the determination to overcome all adversity. After that, she had wandered what had happened to me. Was I OK and did I ever get used to the mouth-piece?

We arranged to meet up and we spoke about our various experiences of life thus far. I recall speaking for a long time, as this new friend of mine was so eager to hear about my illness and the experiences and treatments on the way to recovery. We met again and again, each time exchanging our experiences and always keen to hear what the other had to say.

Here was somebody, who I thought I had never ever seen before and the truth is, I hadn't. She had seen me; not as some strapping man, smooth-talking and well-dressed, but as a hospital patient, battling cancer and struggling to overcome the various obstacles of its aftermath. I had met a lady who was kind, caring and had the utmost empathy for what I had been through and in the short time she had witnessed the workings of the Maxillofacial department, she was really able to relate to my situation.

I stand there looking at the quote and again it communicates with me. 'You wish the cancer had never come to you. You wish that none of this had happened. So do all who live to see such times. But that is not for you to decide. All you have to decide is what to do with the time that is given to you. There are other forces at work in this world, besides the virulent side of cancer. You were meant to have it and that is an encouraging thought.'

Anyone who thinks that we are here today and gone tomorrow, that we are simply floating aimlessly around in the cosmos, without rhyme or reason, that there is no planned schedule to our lives and the lives of the billions of people who are sharing this planet with us, then the concept of destiny or fate, may well be a difficult one to fathom. But if, as I do, you believe that everything that happens to us, does so for a reason, then that can invoke within us feelings of comfort and solace.

The huge number of people I met during the months in and out of hospital, the phone calls I received and continue to receive, from members of the local and wider community, asking for advice, the perspective I can now give to every single event in my life and many of the events in the lives of others. It is because I know what it is like to be told 'Sorry Sir, you have cancer,' to be given high doses of radio and chemotherapy, to have life altering operations, to continuously live with the aftermath of what this dreaded illness leaves behind. But now I can make use of the 'other forces in this world' to encourage people, to give them hope and reassurance. To be in a position where I can truly empathise with someone else and be able to show compassion to every person, regardless of nationality, race or religion. All these negate the 'forces of evil' and that is truly an encouraging thought.

Getting into the Routine and Being Fully Equipped

If any dentist or dental hygienist asks their patient about their 'teeth-cleaning' routine, I suspect the reply will usually include an explanation, somewhere on the scale between very brief and very detailed. Most people, on average, usually spend anywhere between three to five minutes passing their toothbrush around their mouth, trying to access the various crevices and awkward spots in their mouth, where some of their teeth are difficult to reach. The dentist or hygienist will probably retort that the time a person should spend cleaning their teeth is in the region of six minutes.

Most people will tell you that teeth-cleaning becomes a daily routine (preferably a twice-daily routine), which is done automatically after eating breakfast first thing in the morning, during the five minutes still remaining before they have to leave for work. Routine is ever so important to us all and enables the vast majority of adults to perform daily tasks as part of a regular procedure, rather than for a special reason.

A fighter, preparing themselves for a bout or simply maintaining the good physical and mental strengths they have developed over time, will create a routine. They will focus primarily on their strength, their speed, their agility and their psychological prowess.

This routine equips them with the tools they need for the on-going task of maintaining a body and mind which is fighting fit. Whether or not the fighter is preparing for an imminent fight, they will want to ensure that every part of themselves is fully functioning and on top form.

The routine I have developed for maintaining the health of my mouth and all it entails, usually takes me between 25 to 30 minutes in total. After breakfast every morning and last thing at night, I go to the bathroom and lock the door behind me. I prepare the implements I will need, which includes a toothbrush (child's size), sponge brushes, a very small wire brush to floss, two kinds of toothpaste, mouthwash and two sets of tissues. I then feel ready and equipped, to begin the cleaning. I carefully take the obturator out of my mouth and with toothpaste and toothbrush in hand, I clean the mouth-piece, taking special care around the ever-so important clips, which clip on to my existing teeth to keep it in place. During the first few months it was really quite amusing, taking teeth out of my mouth to clean, but I've got used to it now!

So the cleaning process continues, as I once again, toothpaste and toothbrush at the ready, clean the teeth attached to my own gums! I suppose, this part of the overall 25-minute process is usually quicker, as there aren't as many teeth to clean!

Then there is the cavity itself. I will never forget how squeamish I felt when being told that I would have to keep this obscure hole in my face clean. I remember one of the medical professionals at the hospital demonstrating to me, how best to keep the cavity clean and whilst they were explaining it to the best of their ability and I understood it in theory, I was aware that the practical side would have to be one of trial and error.

After I have cleaned my natural teeth, I take a couple of the pink sponge brushes, which look remarkably like the small chewy lollipops I used to buy from local confectionaries as a child and clean the remaining part of the roof of my mouth (the hard palate). Then, with one or two more pink brushes, I venture as far up the cavity as I can and give the hole as thorough a clean as possible. I usually take the small wire brush and clean between each of the teeth which are possible for me to access, after which I brush my teeth once again, this time with toothpaste which is very high in fluoride. I place my obturator back in my mouth and give it one final rinse with mouthwash.

After trying to imagine the lengths I go to, in keeping my mouth and mouth-piece clean, it isn't a wonder that I am always apprehensive before going away from home. Whereas the majority of people are concerned that they have packed all the right clothes and footwear, my anxiety is fuelled by whether or not I have packed all the equipment I will need to keep my mouth and teeth clean.

When a soldier is on the go, away from home and in a hostile area, it is the duty of the army, to keep the soldiers well equipped. As the Second World War neared its end, there were a number of reasons which contributed to Germany's defeat at the hands of the Allies. One contributing factor was a lack of equipment. Germany had sent its troops into the Russian winter without suitable uniforms and to compound this, the German military machine, at the Battle of the Bulge in Western Europe, ran out of fuel for their tanks, resulting in the German army abandoning their machines, burning them and making their way back to Germany on foot.

When any kind of fighter prepares themselves for the on-coming battle, be it in a ring and a fighter's personal battle, or out in the theatre of war, where the future of whole nations are at stake, preparation is a critical component. A boxer's provisions may be comparably insignificant compared to the provisions needed by an entire army, but they are the fighter's vital tools, without which, they are not fully prepared.

I remember taking a large group of 75 school children, aged nine and ten years, away for a weekend to the South coast. As I woke up on the Saturday morning, my face felt unusual and once I had taken a better look at it in the mirror, I realised that it was infected. I had become used to getting infections in the right side of my face and they would present themselves as a swelling, anywhere between my nose and upper lip, right up to my ear. I immediately informed my colleagues that I had to go back to my room to get the antibiotics I had brought away with me and of course they fully understood. I poured myself a glass of water and took the first dose of a seven day course of much needed and effective antibiotics. Not for the first time, I looked and pointed heavenward and felt pleasantly reassured that I had come away from home, equipped with all the essentials.

When I go away from home, I take all the equipment which will see me through to the end of my stay. I pack the toothbrushes, the wire brushes, the mouthwash, the 'lollipop sticks', the toothpastes, the spare obturator and antibiotics, so that I am able to maintain that ever so important routine. Vital equipment is important to fighters, critical to whole armies and essential to me.

Empathy for Others and a Positive Outlook on Life

In my opinion, it is incumbent upon all of us, who have survived our battles with cancer and its aftereffects, to make a positive use of those experiences by touching those around us with a sense of positivity and optimism, in one way or another. I don't just mean friends and family, but every single person with whom we come into contact, be it at work, in the street, in shops, etc. I was once told a story, that not so many years ago in busy New York City, in a supermarket, there was a certain 'bagger'. Let's call him Michael. 'Michael the Bagger'. Michael was known as a 'bagger' because it was his job to help customers pack their bags full of the shopping they had just purchased. Michael was a very simple fellow, who had not done at all well at school and whose understanding of the world was very limited, hence his parents had found him this job, which suited him well.

As Michael would finish packing a customer's bags, handing them to the lady or gentleman shopper, he would leave them with a cheerful greeting. Michael would do this for everyone who passed through the till at which he stood each day, until this routine became a familiar ritual, at check-out number 15, Michael's usual check-out.

Some time elapsed and Michael's father heard about his son's good-will greetings, which seemed to leave customers feeling happy, cheerful and good about themselves. He sat down to write these greetings on small slips of paper and gave them to his son to pass on to customers. Indeed, Michael would pack the bags for a customer and slip a greeting into one of their shopping bags. When the customer arrived home and unpacked their shopping, that slip of paper would be read and it would give an immense feeling of happiness and appreciation to the customer.

After a while, people would stand waiting at Michael's check-out, despite the long queue and even with the knowledge, that ten of the other check-out aisles were virtually empty of customers. Michael's slips of paper had touched the hearts of so many people and had boosted their spirits.

Amongst so many different things, my experiences have taught me the value of making others feel good about themselves. When I go to any cashier in any shop, I make it my duty to greet them cheerfully, always with a smile and they regularly smile back at me. I then always end my brief conversation with a salutation for a good morning, afternoon or evening and if the person at the till wasn't smiling before, they are usually smiling after my very short, but uplifting exchange.

I go through the same process with everyone I meet, at school, at the bus station, in the cinema, everywhere I go.

The great war-time British Prime Minister, Winston Churchill, once said, 'A pessimist sees the difficulty in every opportunity. An optimist sees the opportunity in every difficulty.' My life has changed considerably over the past 15 years and many of my personal experiences have been difficult. However, if I can fly the flag of optimism, in the face of all adversity, then I will continue seeing the opportunity in those difficult situations and experiences and in turn, reach out to others with the same message. As the Dalai Lama once said, 'Happiness is the highest form of health.' So, of course, continue the treatments which the medical experts prescribe and administer, as these are so essential, but a healthy dose of pure happiness will never go amiss.

It is not about winning or losing the fight, but whether or not one has the will to fight and then uses all the strategies at one's disposal. Every single person who has suffered or is suffering with cancer, must adopt and use the 'fighting spirit.'

So hold your head up high, use that 'second wind', deploy every manoeuvre that you know and shout out loud and clear:

'Cancer may have started the fight, but I will do everything in my power to finish it.'